The Andy Griffith Story

The
Andy Griffith
Story

An Illustrated Biography

Written by

Terry Collins

Illustrations by

Bill Neville

PO Box 1907
Mount Airy, NC 27030

1995

Although the author and publisher have made every effort to ensure the accuracy and completeness of information contained in this book, we assume no responsibility for errors, inaccuracies, omissions, or any inconsistency herein. Any slights of people, places, or organizations are unintentional. Please contact the author with any substantiated corrections or new information at the above address for inclusion in later editions of this book.

First Edition. 1995.

ISBN Number   (softcover)   1-887138-01-3
                     (hardcover)   1-887138-00-5

Library of Congress Card Number   95-90187

Library of Congress Cataloging-in-Publication Data

Collins, Terry, 1967—
The Andy Griffith Story: An Illustrated Biography/Terry Collins
          ISBN (pbk)   1-887138-01-3
          ISBN (hbk)   1-887138-00-5

1. Andy Griffith (actor, performer). 2. Television—The Andy Griffith Show. 3. North Carolina.

BIOGRAPHY—Griffith, Andy, 1926—

ATTENTION ORGANIZATIONS AND SCHOOLS: Quantity discounts are available on bulk purchases of this book for educational purposes or fund raising. Special books or book excerpts can also be created to fit specific needs. For information, please contact Explorer Press, P.O. Box 1907, Mount Airy, NC 27030. (910) 789-3099.

ACKNOWLEDGMENTS

Tracing the path of Andy Griffith's life and career has been a rewarding, enlightening, and yes, sometimes frustrating experience. However, there has always been one constant in the discovery of Andy's accomplishments, and that is the love and affection of his fans and supporters met along the way. Without them, this book could not have been written.

The author would like to thank the following:

The respective staffs and personnel of the Mount Airy Public Library, the Surry Arts Council, the Mount Airy Visitor's Center, The Mount Airy News and the High Point Public Library, for providing research materials and photographs.

Steve and Bonnie Martin, and the rest of the gang at Pages Bookstore for their advice and patience. Early on, they were always there when needed, even when the questions were endless.

The many collectors of Andy Griffith and Mayberry memorabilia, who were kind enough to loan documents and items from their personal collections and point the author in new and unexplored directions. Special note must be given to Mike Creech of *The Mayberry Times*, Jim Clark of The Andy Griffith Show Rerun Watchers Club and publisher of *The Bullet*, and Neal Brower, scholar, writer and teacher of the truths to be found within The Andy Griffith Show.

Gary Tilley proved to be an invaluable resource. Through his guidance, I was able to access the experience of both the Surry Community College Small Business Center and The Mount Airy Chamber of Commerce. I owe him a debt of thanks.

Gratitude is expressed for the assistance of Dr. Michele Crews, Charles "Snappy Lunch" Dowell, Jim Dowell, Tim Hampton, Michael Moore, CBS Television, Ed Bohannon of Delmar Printing,

Craig Blankenhorn, Don Stewart, Tara Blomquist, Nancy Freeman, John Richardson, Scott Kniskern, Richard Pini of Father Tree Press/ Warp Graphics, and Mark and Melissa Ellis. Special thanks to good neighbors, Don and Debbie McBride of D&D Exotic Birds, for their willingness to keep an eye on the house...and look after the dogs, Penny, Chico and Jaws.

I'd like to thank my wife, Ginny. Without her encouragement, our dream of producing this book would never have become a reality. She's researcher, proofreader, secretary and critic...and I don't know what I'd do without her. I love her dearly, and this book exists because of her belief in me.

Finally, I would like to acknowledge the financial backers of this project. In the summer of 1993 this small group believed...and their faith and support have led to the successful completion of this book:

Conrad & Lois Ayotte   Mike, Lowanda & Tyler Badgett
Sheree R. Barnard   William W. & Greta M. Boyd
Jim and Sandra Collins   Byron S. Cooke
Ralph & Regina Crabb   Glenn & Nita Everly
Pam Fremon   Bob & Martha Goodwin
Russell R. & Addie S. Hiatt   Leon & Sandra Hutson
Melvin T. Jackson   Keith Johnson
Nancy Bradley Knott   Don & Dale Law
Gertrude Lennox   James R. and Glenda S. Littleton
Elwood S. Long, Jr.   David Michelinie
John Moehlmann   Kenny B. Moles
Bill Neville   Bella Op't Hof
Love D. Smith   Rebecca R. Smith
Steve & Dianne Talley   Jane Taylor
Mr. & Mrs. Ray P. Taylor   Tim R. & Desirae Watson

I appreciate it.

This Book Is Dedicated
In Loving Memory
Of

Hazel M. Law

Harlan "Frosty" Leonard

Raymond A. Smith

Three supporters who passed on before the story was completed. We regret they did not see the finished project, but we honor their spirit.

INTRODUCTION

Andy Griffith. The very mention of the name causes a grin of recognition.

Everybody likes Andy. His face can be seen on television screens on a daily basis, either as Andy Taylor or Ben Matlock. Sometimes, he visits in the guise of innocent Will Stockdale or corrupt Lonesome Rhodes. Over the years, he's gone by the names Able Marsh, Andy Sawyer, Harry Broderick, Andy Thompson, Noah Talbot, and numerous other aliases.

Television comes into our homes and provides the illusion of one-on-one. He's been a sheriff, a judge, a mayor and a lawyer...authority figures all. We take comfort in his presence. We feel as though we know Andy.

But do we really?

A private individual, Andy has always kept his own affairs close. His first wife is deceased, his second out of the public's eye, and his third at his side since their marriage in 1983. His two adopted children are now adults, but little is known about them beyond their names.

We know Andy's six feet tall. He has blue eyes and blondish-brown curly hair that has turned a vibrant silver with age. His smile is infectious, but he can turn it off and replace it with a gaze that can pierce steel.

He's a lifelong Democrat, campaigning for North Carolina Governors Jim Hunt and Terry Sanford. He cares deeply for animals and has always had a dog by his side. He enjoys collecting antiques: old furniture, clocks, watches, hats and canes.

He maintains a fleet of classic cars that would put fellow celebrity collector Jay Leno to shame, and close friends and relatives receive a new Christmas card each year adorned with a photo of Andy and family standing in front of one of his autos. Yet, he has never been one to invite a camera crew into his home to show off his automotive trophies.

He allows himself small souvenirs from his work. He still has a few of the Sheriff Taylor uniforms and one of the badges. He keeps a copy of every script of any project of consequence he has done. His home in Manteo is lined with photographs tracing his life and career.

He established a scholarship at the University of North Carolina at Chapel Hill in 1972 with a gift of $25,000. The scholarship is awarded to one (or more) sophomores, juniors or seniors majoring in dramatic art or music who have displayed excellence, and, keeping his own background in mind... have shown need of financial assistance.

But still, behind the wide grin and engaging manner seen on screen, the person behind the roles is more reserved, withdrawn... some even say aloof. Griffith's mind is always working and he never forgets a kindness or a slight. He demands loyalty and when received, he gives it in return.

His work gives us pleasure, reassures us, and offers us escape. He is a good man... and a good actor.

This book was not written to be a definitive biography. We can only offer glimpses into the triumphs and the struggles that went into the making of one of America's favorite actors. The whole story can only come from one man, himself a writer of some skill... and his name is Andy Griffith.

"What I would like to do, whenever I act or entertain, is to say some small truth. No preaching—just have some small thing to say that is true."

—Andy Griffith

In a rented house on South Street in Mount Airy, North Carolina, Andy Samuel Griffith was born on June 1, 1926. He was the first—and only—child of proud parents Carl Lee and Geneva Nann Nunn Griffith. Both parents were of Welsh-English stock, and their mutual strong bloodlines mingled into the creation of their son.

Baby Andy had a pair of striking blue eyes peering out of a face topped off with light blond hair. There was also a birthmark on the back of his head. His mother told him she had seen a strawberry patch right before he was born, and she always called the mark "Andy's Strawberry Patch."

As an adult, the hair would darken, growing out into an unruly wavy brown mop—covering the "strawberry patch" and sitting atop a face that was handsome in the line of nose and jaw, but unassuming and... almost comical in some ways. A friendly face.

Andy's mother doted on her boy from day one. "She was (always) enormously frightened that something would happen to me," Andy said.

Times were tough for the Griffiths, and a new mouth to feed meant added expenses for a family who couldn't even afford a crib for their newborn son; young Andy slept in a drawer from a bureau until he outgrew it. The Griffiths lived with the Moore family— Geneva's sister Grace, her husband John, and their children. The Moores had found room for their kin in the wooden converted barn they were renting, but a new body meant even less space.

1

Carl was a skilled carpenter who had never lacked for work, but living in such a small community meant a limited number of jobs to go around, so the couple decided to move to Ohio with their new addition and stay with Geneva's mother.

The Griffiths were apart from their home state for roughly three years before returning, first to High Point (even then a major furniture manufacturing site and a place where Carl's skills were appreciated) and then back to the Granite City of Andy's birth, where they lived in the Highland Park section of town for a short time before moving back in with Geneva's sister in a new house on Rockford Street.

Carl was weary of traveling and depending on relatives for a place to live. While he was grateful for their aid, he longed to provide a real home for his wife and son. Andy was growing older and would soon start attending school. So, he and his wife saved their money, and eventually were able to buy a house on Haymore Street for $435. No more paying rent. Andy was six years old and the Griffiths were in Mount Airy to stay.

The new home was kept tidy by Geneva, and in excellent repair by Carl, whose skill with wood only got better with age. He was a master of the band saw, specializing in the creation of tables and chairs... and even slingshots for his son. Eventually, Carl would go on to become a foreman for the Mount Airy Chair Company, where he stayed until he retired at the age of 65.

For entertainment, the family listened to an old Majestic radio, over which, in addition to the daily comedy and dramas, was heard lots of country and gospel music. Andy has stated that his mother's family was always musically inclined, while his father's family had a great sense of humor.

"His daddy was a great joker," noted Andy's first cousin Evin Moore, who lived with the family in the early years. "There was never any dark moments with Carl Griffith."

Andy's mother and father were also entertainers, in their own way. Andy received his first training in music from his mother, who showed him simple chords on the guitar; while his father is remembered as being a true storyteller in the Carolina upland tradition.

Out of the house, there were movies, and even live theatre now and then.

"The first show I ever saw was when I was five and my daddy and mother took me to Winston-Salem, about thirty-five miles away (from Mount Airy), to see a road-company production of *Carmen*. All that clapping and clanging and carrying on! I sure did enjoy it!" Andy once said.

Griffith's first wife once commented that she thought the true source of Andy's humor was a subconscious desire to caricature his father, whom she believed to be one of the funniest men she'd ever known.

"I think my father had an enormous influence on me," Andy has often said. "He was a Christian man, truly honorable and honest, a fine human being, and he had a magnificent sense of humor.... If he could've had a chance, he would've been a really fine actor."

Humor was needed by families during this period in the United States. The Depression stretched across the country, and although on a much smaller scale, Mount Airy was affected just as much as larger cities. Many men were out of work and their families were hungry, but Carl Griffith persevered:

"Growing up in Mount Airy, we were poor people, but we were not in poverty. All during the Depression—almost all the time—my father had a job somewhere. If our factory shut down, he would find one somewhere that was open. He was good at running a band saw, so he'd get the job."

While still young, Andy began to work beside his father in the factories after school. Andy was a dreamer, but at the same time possessed the drive of a hard worker—if the work suited him. He knew making chairs wasn't going to be his career and he recalled his dislike of working in the furniture factory in a 1990 article for *Parade Magazine*:

"When I was real young, I didn't much like to work... I didn't like to pull a cross saw and throw wood under the house and things like that. What I did like was listening to *The Lone Ranger*. When I was working in a factory with my father—and I *hated*, working in the factory—work took up at a quarter 'til eight, and we shut down at a quarter 'til five. Now, *The Lone Ranger* came on at five, Monday, Wednesday and Friday, and we'd just be draggin' along.

"Finally, Dad would say, 'We'd better hurry up. We're gonna miss *The Lone Ranger*.' So we'd sit together by the radio, and Dad would do the same thing every time. When some character'd say, 'Who was that masked man?' Then the other person would say, 'That was the L-o-n-e Ranger,' and you'd hear, 'Hiyo, Silver, away!' My father'd go, 'Whooooeee!'

"Or, if something really astounded him, or if he saw a really pretty woman, he'd do a whole body take, go 'Whoooeee!' and he'd walk out of the room and come back and do it again. Even now, periodically I... do a body take or make that sound, just like my dad did."

As much as Andy disliked making chairs, he thought even less of school. Never a good student, Griffith was held back a year after failing spelling and arithmetic. According to Andy's cousin, Glenn

Thacker, the story was that "they kept Andy in Dora Valentine's third-grade class for two years.... His mother told him Dora Valentine kept him there because she liked him so much."

Actually, Thacker neglected to mention that Griffith also suffered through a series of childhood diseases when he was nine years old. Between the mumps and chicken pox—and his mother's fretfulness—Andy was absent from school for days on end. Ultimately, he missed enough to be kept back.

Geneva Griffith tended to be overprotective of her child, hovering over him constantly throughout Andy's youth. However, he was devoted to her in turn. For a family so close, even the smallest gestures meant a lot. One time, when Andy was just a child he walked by himself to a downtown Mount Airy florist and purchased his mother a gift with his own money. He presented Geneva with a small potted plant—the only thing he could afford—and it set his mother to crying for three days.

Still, as an adult Andy recalled growing up in Mount Airy as "fun." He was a good boy, but absent-minded. According to his cousin Evin Moore, Andy was prone to lose things, coats mainly. Then there was the time he forgot about the pocketful of tar he'd left in a good pair of pants.

"One time Andy figured to lay in a supply of tar. It melted, ruined his pants, he got you-know-what-for," Moore remembered. "It's just like chewing gum. But we didn't have no money for chewing gum."

City road crews would blacktop the roads during the hot summer months, giving children a steady supply of the black goo. However, even when he came home covered in sticky tar, Andy was never spanked by his parents. They kept a strict household, but it was tempered with respect, not anger.

Andy was not an athlete, and was too shy to skinny-dip at the local swimming hole, which the kids called "Little Slippy." Friends remember him as being someone who could always diffuse a situation with humor — a natural talent brought forth early in Griffith's childhood:

"In school I was the patsy that everyone picked on. They would hold me down and call me Andy Gump and Amos and Andy. And I hated, hated, hated it — but at some point, my child's mind recognized that I could control the kind of fun that was being made of me. In this way, it put me in charge of the laughter. So I grew up as a class clown; it was a defense mechanism."

Another time, Andy remarked: "I guess it took me a long time to find out what I wanted to do. I always looked for a way to function as an individual person. But I started out a loser. Believe me, I was convinced I was born that way by the time I reached adulthood.

"I wasn't smart, my family wasn't wealthy and I wasn't athletic. In a little town like Mount Airy, if you aren't wealthy or athletic you *aren't much.* You know what I mean? I had to find something else for myself, something mine."

Griffith remembers himself as being a "little old white-headed boy" who was wily enough to take his flair for entertaining and turn it into an advantage. A twice-yearly school assembly at the Rockford Street Grammar School provided one of his earliest audiences.

There are two versions of Andy's first public appearance and Andy himself has given both versions to interviewers over the years.

One version of the story had Andy daring a pal to get up on stage with him and sing a duet of "Put On Your Old Gray Bonnet." Of course, Andy only knew the chorus, but he didn't let that stop him. However, when the duo was to make their debut, Andy was the only one to appear.

6

He took one look at the audience, stood proudly with his hands behind his back and let 'er rip, singing through the chorus twice— one time slow and a second time fast. The auditorium came apart with laughter, and Andy realized that while he was being laughed at (and this wasn't the first time), for once, he was in control of the situation.

The second version of the story also comes directly from the source himself in a frank 1963 interview:

"When I was a kid, back in Mount Airy, North Carolina, the other fellas—and worse, the girls—used to laugh at me. It seemed to me they laughed at me all the time. Not with me, mind you, but at me. My mama made me wear long underwear, and when we had to change in the gym, the other guys would double over in hysterics. It finally got so I'd dress in the shower or toilet where they couldn't see me... I was an awful shy, scraggly, homely kid, and I'd fall over imaginary objects and trip myself up with my own big feet. I wanted to belong like the rest of the kids, but I was too embarrassed to express myself or my needs. I don't even think I knew what my needs were. There were times when I thought I just wanted to die.

"The happiest times I spent were in my room by myself, where no one could jeer or poke fun at me. And then it happened. That chance to make something out of a handicap that so many people let pass by. One day I was a kid with a big hurt, a complex you could see coming a mile away, and then—I said something funny. I made a whole room full of people laugh. They laughed at me, but all of a sudden I was in control because I'd *made* them laugh.

"That was a long time ago, but I've never forgotten the lesson. As long as everyone was going to laugh at me, anyway, I might as well put myself in the position where I could control the laughter. I turned a disadvantage into an advantage, and in doing it, I changed my whole life.

7

"This other kid, Albert McKnight—and I'll never forget his name to my dying day—was in my homeroom at the Rockford Street Grammar School, and we sat next to each other in weekly assembly. Someone from each class was always assigned to represent his room and get up and do something, and the teacher had chosen Albert to recite a poem we'd learned in English class.

"When the principal announced that the next offering would be heard from our homeroom, I was sitting on the aisle, and I got up to let Albert out. And you know what he did? He just sat there like an idiot and smirked up at me. There I was, the only one standing up in that big auditorium, and I realized Albert and the rest of my room were just putting me on.

"I don't know to this day what made me do it... I guess I was just plumb tired of being made a fool of. But I marched up to the stage and started reciting the poem we'd learned. In between the lines, I'd make little comments of my own on what I thought of the poem and the person who wrote it, and they started laughing. I found out I could get them to laugh or listen whenever I wanted them to. What an experience—that great sea of laughter.

"From that time on, no one kidded me because they knew I could whip them verbally. And, most important, I knew it.... A lot of us, most of us, I guess, had unhappy experiences as kids, and the secret is not to just overcome them, but to make the most of them. After all, experience is a dead loss if you can't sell it for more than it cost you. You know what I mean?"

However, Andy's childhood wasn't all confrontational. Many good times were spent with friends like Emmett Forrest, Douglas Benison or Garnett Steele fishing for perch in Lovill's Creek and playing Kick the Can—or sitting on the curb under the streetlight at the corner of Rockford and Broad Streets with other neighborhood boys and girls telling ghost stories late into the night.

Griffith has spoken of "... The fun we kids had in the summer kicking rocks and lying to each other in that wonderful, sloweddown time between dusk and dark" during his boyhood days.

He had a bicycle he rode everywhere—to school, to church, and back home. Up and down he pedaled, riding along the unpaved Mount Airy streets. Sometimes, he carried a passenger—his little brown and white dog, Tippy—in the wire basket on the handlebars.

Other times, if not outdoors, he could be found at home concentrating on building one of the many model airplanes that dotted his small room... or dreading an overnight visit from kinfolk. Sleeping accommodations at the Griffith home were limited, and Andy would end up having to sleep on the floor.

Andy was raised a Baptist, and most of his early social life revolved around the church, where he was to eventually join the Baptist Young People's Union and do his "early courting."

However, Andy still desired to fit in as an athlete. As a freshman at Mount Airy High School, he made one more attempt:

"I went out for basketball my freshman year. I was third team center and they put me in a game one time and somebody threw that ball to me and I don't know where it went! It scared me to death, and the next morning I was on the fifth team and that ended my basketball career."

At the age of 15, the teenager traveled down to Mount Airy's theatre row on Main Street and saw *Birth Of The Blues*, a movie starring Bing Crosby and Mary Martin. Andy had developed a love of swing music. He loved big bands, going to every movie that featured one. In *Birth*, his attention was drawn to Jack Teagarden's expert playing of a trombone in the film. The shiny horn imbedded itself into Griffith's memory.

"I'd been asking for a musical instrument of some kind, but my daddy couldn't afford it; he fed me and clothed me, but he couldn't stretch his pay far enough to buy me (one)," Griffith stated about those early days. The teenager did have a harmonica, but was ready to expand his musical horizons. While relatives on his mother's side could play guitar and banjo, they couldn't help Andy with the instrument he desired to learn.

Griffith watched Jack Teagarden take a trombone apart in the film, and follow up his repair work by putting a glass over the end of the slide. This ignited the musical spark when Teagarden started playing a tune—it made Andy realize he wanted to be a musician.

In order to pay for music lessons and instruments, Griffith took a job courtesy of President Roosevelt's NYA (National Youth Administration) sweeping out rooms at Mount Airy High School after classes. The salary was small, a mere $6 a month, but gave him enough to make monthly payments on a used and reconditioned $33 trombone seen advertised in a well-thumbed Spiegel mail-order catalog.

A teenaged Andy in his Sunday best

"I lied about my age for (the job). I was just 15," Andy later admitted. "It took me five and a half months, but then I got this trombone and I was the happiest boy in all of North Carolina. It was a tenor trombone — silver plated. Then, I started looking around for someone to teach me how to play it."

In his immediate circle, no one could help. Mount Airy High School had no school band and there were no private teachers.

10

"It was the most beautiful thing I'd ever owned. For two months I admired it and polished it and wondered what to do with it because there was nobody in our town to teach music," Andy remembered. "Then I heard about this minister with the Moravian Church some miles away. People said he knew all about music—he could tune an organ; matter of fact, he'd installed the organ at that church."

Enter Edward Timothy Mickey, a Moravian minister and musician who had recently arrived to serve in Mount Airy. His duties included overseeing the Moravian Youth Church Band, which was made up entirely of brass instruments —a fact not lost on Andy, who wasted no time in asking the preacher for lessons.

Andy arrived before the weary Mickey on a Wednesday afternoon. The minister was sitting on the outdoor basement steps after a frustrating session of trying to teach a dozen unrehearsed band members how to play a simple song... but no one had practiced or even appeared to care how bad they sounded.

And now this blond kid on a bicycle had shown up to bother him.

"You the preacher here?" Andy asked.

Mickey said yes, and asked Andy how he could help. When Andy told Mickey he wanted to learn how to play a horn, the minister groaned.

"Why do you want to learn to play a horn?" Mickey asked.

"So I can lead a swing band," Andy announced. He told the minister he wanted to play a slide trombone. Mickey breathed a sigh of relief, thinking he had discovered an out since he had no idea how to play that particular instrument. He told his aspiring student all he could do would be to go through an instruction book... if the boy happened to have one... ?

Andy cheerfully told the minister he had an instruction book... and yes, before Mickey could ask the next question, he already had his own instrument. "Bought it from Spiegel," Andy said.

"Well, I couldn't get rid of him, so I said, 'Come back next Wednesday and we'll see,' " Mickey remembered. "I figured coming two miles across town on a bicycle carrying that trombone he wouldn't last long."

However, Mickey hadn't counted on Griffith's tenacity. The next Wednesday afternoon found a trombone-toting Andy standing before the minister and waiting for his first lesson. Mickey kept the instruction book to look over, and sent Andy home with a scale written on a piece of paper.

The following Wednesday, Andy was waiting... and had the scale note perfect. More weeks followed, and the student would arrive with his assignment memorized and wanting to learn more. Mickey increased the length of the lessons and Andy kept up effortlessly... or so it seemed.

Finally, Mickey asked where the boy was getting the time to practice and Andy responded proudly, "Well, I tell you: I've got my school work and I've got my studying and I've got my paper route and I've got my church work.... And that doesn't leave me much time, so I've been getting up about five o'clock in the morning to practice!"

With this kind of dedication, Mickey's doubts vanished. He put his young protégé in the Moravian band, where Andy quickly picked up the fingering of the other horns. The baritone horn, B-flat alto, bass horn, valve trombone... Andy learned how to pick out melodies on all of them.

"His enthusiasm sparked enthusiasm in the other band members. About the third week, I began to see the boy had more determination in him than a passing fancy," Mickey said.

"For three years, he gave me a free lesson once a week. Ed Mickey taught me to sing and to read music and to play every brass instrument there was in the band... he also talked me into studying voice and I wound up singing solos all over Mount Airy.... I asked (Mickey) how much it was going to be and he said, 'I'll charge nothing.' I'll never forget that," Griffith later wrote in an essay about his beginnings in the entertainment business.

"When I was 16, I joined the (Moravian) church, together with my mother and daddy. We had been Baptists, but it was all Protestant anyhow, so it didn't make any difference. I was very happy with the Moravians. All the other band members accepted me," Andy remembered.

Griffith has also remembered that many citizens of Mount Airy were supportive of him at this time, offering words of encouragement and even the occasional small amount of money to help the gangly teenager make ends meet. Mickey had tried to interest him in singing in the church choir, but Andy thought that would be too sissy.

Finally, after repeated encouragement from the minister (who started his pupil off slow with a short religious song called "The Prayer Perfect"), Andy was soon an in-demand singer and soloist.

"(Mickey) taught me to sing.... Well, then it really turned around, because I sang all over Mount Airy—everywhere. The joy that brought me made me know that I had to pursue it," Andy said.

When performing music, Griffith found all of his anxieties disappeared. "Andy wasn't bashful about singing in front of people," Glenn Thacker remembered. "I remember when he got on-stage and did 'On the road to Mandalay, where the flyin' fishes play.' You'd break out in chill-bumps when he sang. He had a stirring voice."

A strong bass in numerous church and school choruses, the young musician housed secret fantasies of becoming a great opera singer—a fantasy fueled by repeated viewings of Ezio Pinza in the film *A Night At Carnegie Hall*. Pinza sang the great operatic role of Boris Godunov in the movie, and Andy dreamed more than once of singing the same role.

However, the same boy who dreamed of being an opera singer could usually be found during this period at a part-time job working as a soda jerk at the Wiener-Burger restaurant for his cousin Evin. According to Evin, Andy was no cook, but he could make hot dogs and milk shakes. Primarily, they kept Andy away from the stove and at the sink washing dishes.

After work, Andy might show up booming out lyrics to a non-sense song he'd written to sing while he and the other young people involved in the Moravian Church Band did their weekly chore of cleaning the church.

This task was accomplished with lots of hard work, soap and water, and remnants of cloth donated by Spencer's, Inc., a local Mount Airy baby clothes manufacturer. The free cloth inspired Andy to start singing "Wash your windows with Dr. Spencer's Underwear." According to his fellow band member Jessie Mae Pruett Jones, this song had several verses, which Andy would make up as he cleaned the stained glass windows.

"(Andy) played the slide trombone and I the cornet for special church services," remembered Mrs. Jones. "Andy also taught me to play the bass drum for the ice cream socials held on the church lawn, and for when we played marches. There were five of us young people from that band who played from the back of a truck, traveling up and down Main Street. The truck had banners on the sides, and on Saturdays we rode up and down the street, drumming up a crowd of people for land auctions. We were paid five dollars each which we used to buy more band instruments and sheet music for the band and for the church choir."

"We didn't have a school band nor a school glee club then and that's why music meant so much to me—because I became worth something. I could do something besides struggle to get C's in my classes," Andy said.

However, since there was no high school choral group, Andy's vocal talents were unknown to most of his fellow classmates at Mount Airy High School. Fellow high school graduate and class president Robert Merritt recalled how shocked the class was at a banquet held at the end of the senior year when Andy agreed to sing a number:

"In high school, Andy never attracted much attention, as far as I can remember. Nothing in his manner suggested a career in acting... (but) about halfway through the program... Andy sang 'Long Ago And Far Away.' During a moment of stunned silence, somebody expressed our surprise by exclaiming 'Gollee, ol' Ange can sing!' Long and enthusiastic applause followed. He... consented to an encore, and another one. We might have kept him going all evening but for a cooler head.... Years later, I was not surprised at his success on stage—his secret had leaked out in a few magical minutes in 1944."

But Andy was a realist. Singing was fun, he loved it, but he knew he couldn't hope to make a living as a vocalist. No, Andy believed his future career was of another kind of calling—a calling that would allow him to continue to sing while working in the church and showing his love of the Lord.

Through his continuing participation with the Moravians, and because of Reverend Mickey's influence, Andy was interested in becoming even more involved with the church. Mickey told his young pupil that college would have to be a part of Andy's future if the young man was serious about a career in the ministry.

Andy was serious, and began to harbor plans of going to school and becoming a minister.

After Mickey was called to serve another church in the state, Andy assumed leadership of the Moravian band until a new preacher arrived. Some thought the preacher was already in place, and remarked to Griffith that he was the new pastor as far as they were concerned.

Griffith liked the sound of that, so, after singing a farewell solo at the graduation exercises for Mount Airy High School at the Rockford Street School Auditorium and picking up his diploma on May 30, 1944, he enrolled that fall at the University of North Carolina at Chapel Hill as a pre-ministerial student.

"... I went to college to be a Moravian preacher," Andy told Cleveland Amory in 1967. "The tradition of that church is musical. They have lovely services and it's all based on loving one another. They even have one service called a 'Love Feast.' The women serve coffee and buns and you sing hymns; that's all there is to it. But the most beautiful of all is the Easter Sunrise service. It starts at three in the morning—that's when we'd go to blowing.

"We'd ride around on the back of a truck with our trumpets and trombones waking everybody up and then we'd all go to the church yard and just wait. And then, just as the sun started to crack, the preacher would come out of the church. He'd be all dressed in white and everything would be very quiet. 'The Lord is risen,' he'd say. 'The Lord has risen indeed.' And then we'd march to the graveyard and sing hymns. Some were quiet and some were jubilant, but they were all beautiful."

The first person Andy met in Chapel Hill was Edwin S. Lanier, the self-help officer for the school. He got the student a job as a busboy in the campus cafeteria. Payment was free breakfast and $8 a week: $5 for tuition and $3 to live on. Although strapped financially, Griffith took considerable pride at being a freshman at the university. He was the first in his family on either side to ever attend college, and he knew their hopes and dreams had traveled to Chapel Hill with him.

The constant work and time spent on his studies took their toll on the young Griffith. A sound sleeper, Andy knew better than to trust a clock, so he came up with the simple solution of tying a piece of rope around one ankle and lowering the other end out of his second floor dormitory window.

Andy in college

All of his friends knew about the rope, and when early morning classes began, it was each and every person's duty to tug the rope when passing by until Andy came to the window and said he was up.

The rope worked, until late one night when a group of his pals walked past from a party. They spotted Andy's makeshift alarm clock dangling down and decided to have their buddy join them— so four or five guys took the rope and heaved as hard as they could.

As a result, the sound-asleep Andy shot out of bed and straight through the open window, awakening just in the nick of time to grab the window sill and hang on to keep himself from falling.

The rope alarm was retired after Andy's midnight trip.

Andy's freshman year was spent studying for the ministry and taking the required classes in sociology. However, he soon discovered he disliked sociology to the point where he walked out and took an F. The same applied to his studies of Latin and Greek, where he found the classes "long and dull." Psychology was no better. He tried to apply himself and use good study habits, but usually spent long hours staring at his text books and walking away without retaining any of what he had read.

"I failed Political Science 41 twice," Andy wrote in 1983 in an essay for *The UNC-CH Report*. "My counselor, a lady, called me in and said: 'Andy, very few people fail political science once, but nobody fails it twice.' I guess that was the only record I ever broke at Chapel Hill."

Missing his music, Andy went to Bishop Pfhol, who was the Bishop of the Southern Province of the Moravian Church, and told him how he felt. "I asked him if I could major in music instead of sociology. He said that, unfortunately, music was not a base for the ministry. That was it," Griffith said.

Andy approached his former mentor Ed Mickey with the news.

" 'I've changed my major to music,' I told him, and he was very kind. He simply said, 'I had a notion you would.' "

In later years, Andy admitted that if he had attended a Moravian College, he probably would have gone on to become a minister, bad grades or not. However, being at Chapel Hill gave him other choices... and when he embraced these opportunities they changed his life.

Andy returned to his old specialty of brass instruments and started with slide trombone in the college band. He was third chair trombone, and wasn't progressing since the music was giving him problems. So, he went to the band director and asked about the E-flat bass sousaphone instead.

The director was delighted. Sousaphone players were hard to come by and the instrument became one of the student's specialties, although he was to later state: "I was never meant to be a fine musician. I had no patience for all the practice. I just played melody."

Then, a chronic back problem that went back to a childhood injury when he fell from a rope swing returned to plague Andy. He went to Duke Medical for an examination, and what an X ray of his back revealed was not promising:

"They told me (my back) was all out of line and I'd have to wear a brace, a big old leather thing with steel running up and down. It cost thirty dollars, so I went to Mr. Lanier to see if I could get my tuition deferred. He wrote down a man's name and.... The man's name was W. Rea Parker, and (Mr. Parker) got me talking right off about what I wanted to do with my life.

"He couldn't understand how a man with a major in music would make a living, but he told me the state of North Carolina had a program for indigent students with physical disabilities and that they would help me out with my tuition and a few books.... when I asked him how I was expected to pay back the money, all he said was: 'You get a good education, a good job, and be a good tax-payer.' Well, there are a lot of things I haven't done in my life. But I did get my education, I do have a good job, and I've been a wonderful taxpayer."

His back problems and immediate financial needs taken care of, Andy began singing in the campus glee club. He also looked into the opportunities available in the Drama Department, where a group called the Carolina Playmakers put on an operetta once a year — usually Gilbert and Sullivan. Andy didn't know who Gilbert and Sullivan were, but after seeing a notice posted about auditions he decided to find out.

"I auditioned to get into the chorus, if I could (singing the old church standard 'Shepherds See Thy Horse's Foaming Mane') and was lucky enough to get the role of Don Alhambra del Bolero, the Grand Inquisitor, in *The Gondoliers*. When the review of the show came out in the school paper, my performance was referred to as the best. From that moment on, I was in every musical show they produced."

"(Andy had) a nice, loud, strong voice, but I don't know how good it was," remembered Foster Fitz-Simons, the director of Andy's campus acting debut. "But I realized right away I had something. I told my wife to come down and have a look."

What Marion Fitz-Simons saw was that Griffith had an immediate rapport with the audience and a sharp comic talent impossible to ignore. Andy went on to sing most of the comedy leads from Gilbert and Sullivan, along with the bass arias in Haydn's *The Seasons*, and "The People Who Walk In Darkness" from *The Messiah*.

"The first play I ever did was... directed by Foster Fitz-Simons," Andy wrote of his early days. "A fine, fine man who took extra effort and time and care with me. He brought people over to give me encouragement, special people like Sam Selden, Kai Jurgensen, and Marion Fitz-Simons, herself a fine actor, who made me feel like I was ten feet tall when she talked to me."

Andy acted every chance he got. "In college," he later remembered, "whenever I got in a play, it totally consumed me. I never thought about anything else and I didn't go to class."

Paul Young, head of the university choral department, also took an interest in the young performer. He told Andy that if he was going to be a singer, he needed to study voice. When Andy told him that he couldn't pay for private lessons or classes, Young told Griffith not to worry.

If Andy would work as a music librarian and maintain the

20

music books of the Glee Club, Young would teach him for nothing. Andy was to study with Young for five years. Later, he said: "It was hard for me.... Most people who make music have been involved in music since they were young, real young. But I did it...."

However, even with his numerous social activities, Andy still felt inadequate and self-conscious as he walked around the Carolina college campus. He loved the school, but was "scared to death... for fear of being found out for not knowing, for not having studied." The only place where he was able to rid himself of such feelings was when he was acting or singing.

The fledgling actor could also be found traveling back and forth to Mount Airy to play roles in productions staged by the Mount Airy Operetta Club in the Rockford Street School Auditorium. First, he hitchhiked home to play the judge in the Gilbert and Sullivan operetta *Trial By Jury* in 1945.

Then, in November, 1946, Andy was back to portray Kezal, a village marriage broker in the comic opera *The Bartered Bride*, which was produced and directed by Clifford E. Bair, the President of the National Opera Association.

The Bartered Bride was an important show for the club thanks to Bair's involvement. His name gave the opera an added element of class. Bair was present for four of the five November performances, but he missed an afternoon matinee given to 700 bored school children.

The curtain rose on the first act of the production. After an hour or so, the young audience became restless... until a cast member hit a high note and caused a window shade of a 25-foot window to snap loose, fly to the top, and flop loudly on its spool. The kids promptly responded with a loud burst of laughter.

Comedian Andy, who was on stage with fellow actor Jim Bray was supposed to exit at Bray's side. However, Andy couldn't resist and leaped on Bray's back to be carried into the wings by piggy back. More laughter from the children, who applauded Andy as he waved good-bye.

Bray recalled the matinee as being "A most enjoyable, if not the most professional performance.... Those were the days! Andy's humor was evident...."

Andy also joined the cast of the outdoor historical pageant *The Lost Colony*, in the summer of 1946. Paul Green's historical epic was staged annually on Roanoke Island in Manteo, North Carolina to commemorate the exploration of the site of the first English colony in the New World of America, which was established under Sir Walter Raleigh. Later, while Raleigh was away, the colony vanished under mysterious and still unexplained circumstances.

For seven summers, Andy lived with his fellow actors in the buildings of a deserted Navy air base built during World War II. Because none of the young actors had cars, they rode to work each day in an old rattle-trap of a school bus. Andy was making $25 a week, but living in a vacation paradise. "... We didn't hurt for anything," Andy once said. "We had our own swimming hole, our own beach. It was the best time I ever had."

As the summers passed, Andy went from bit parts of five lines to supporting roles and understudy for Raleigh. Finally, for the last five of his seven-year association with the pageant, Griffith took the lead role of Sir Walter Raleigh himself.

"They let me understudy until they thought I was old enough to play it. I never was very good at it," Andy claimed. "I never was."

On one occasion, while playing Sir Walter, Griffith overheard two ladies talking. One commented to the other about Andy's "spindly legs." Griffith promptly rushed right out and got some cotton wadding (other nights he used newspaper), which he then packed into his stockings. "I just had to give myself some good-looking legs," he later laughed.

Andy's pilgrimages to Manteo during his college years were to have a lasting impact. The boy from the mountains had never seen the ocean before, and he was hypnotized. His love of the North Carolina seashore and the people who lived there, was to remain a

Andy as Sir Walter Raleigh in Paul Green's **The Lost Colony**

constant in his life. "I actually became an entertainer here so this place is very meaningful to me. In a sense," he once said. "I grew up here."

He spent much of his time in Manteo with his friend Ainslie Pryor, who gave Andy encouragement when the actor began experimenting on Saturday nights at the Beach Club in Nags Head with embryonic versions of his later famed comedy monologues.

"Those wonderful people from Dare County. They laughed when the monologues were funny, and they forgave me when they weren't. But the people came anyway... They gave me a chance to search for something—and to find it," Andy said about his first attempts.

"... I put together an act that included off-color announcements, songs and a sermon called 'The Preacher And The Bear.' I performed the act... one summer. I would shout out the sermon and I would get the audience to yelling 'Amen' and all that. Then I would do a hymn called 'In The Pines' and stomp my foot. I never have known why that was funny, but they would just go crazy."

So, he now had a routine about a foot-stomping southern preacher, who dressed in a split-tailed coat and shared the stage with a choir of gospel singers (recruited from *The Lost Colony* cast), but Andy was interested in going beyond the call and response of "The Preacher Act" and attempting something a bit more... literary.

"I wanted to do something on Shakespeare, but I just couldn't get anywhere with it. And so I called my friend R.G. Armstrong... (and) said, 'Bob, how about coming over here and telling me the story of *Hamlet*? Well, he did, and I got it all down and fooled with it. And that was the first one," Andy said.

When he tried his country version of *Hamlet* out on the agreeable audiences in Nags Head, Andy got huge laughs in return. "I told it that night as a man from the mountains of North Carolina might tell it to his friends. And it worked."

Soon after graduating in June of 1949 with a degree in Music (Voice), Griffith married his first wife, Barbara Bray Edwards. The couple had met back in 1946 in the Carolina Playmakers. Both were auditioning for an oratorio. Both won solos.

A tall, intelligent brunette, Barbara was the daughter of a Troy, NC school superintendent. Like her husband, the green-eyed singer was a music major and accomplished actor. A dramatic soprano, she had received her degree from Converse College at Spartanburg, South Carolina.

Reportedly, Andy was so smitten, he proposed three days after they met—but when he first heard about his future wife, he was under the impression she was a he. Andy thought she was another bass-baritone to match voices against.

The college was preparing a Spring presentation of Haydn's *The Seasons* and Andy wanted a spot. A mutual friend noted that Andy might be up for some tough competition from "Bobby Edwards."

"I don't know him," Andy said. "I don't know any Bobby Edwards."

"The 'Bobby' is short for Barbara, and she's quite a gal," Andy was told, and after seeing her, Andy was in total agreement.

Then he heard her sing... and Andy knew she was the one for him. They were soon inseparable, spending all their free time together. Barbara even traveled with Andy to Manteo, where she also joined the cast of *The Lost Colony*.

After their courtship, Barbara agreed to become Mrs. Griffith and a date was chosen. Because they had Monday evenings off from the play, the wedding ceremony was celebrated at eleven o'clock on the morning of August 22, 1949. The couple were married in the Little Log Chapel in Manteo.

Referring to the interdenominational aspects of his marriage, Griffith has said he was "Married in a copy of an Anglican chapel... by a Methodist minister, to a Baptist maiden, while a Roman Catholic vibraphonist played the pump organ."

An octet from Westminster Choir sang, and after a turn at the pump organ, Sal Razassi played "Ave Maria" on his vibraharp.

"You wouldn't expect a vibraharp to be effective—or maybe even ecclesiastical—but I've never heard the 'Ave Maria' played with greater solemnity. It was the sort of thing you can never forget," Andy said about the music performed on his wedding day.

Andy and Barbara enjoy a break from **The Lost Colony**

However, the summer was over, and the Griffiths' performing jobs were about to end—at least, until next year, and they both knew three months of steady work were not enough to provide means for a family.

Luckily, Andy was in the right place at the right time. Clifton Britton, the stage manager of *The Lost Colony*, knew of a job opening. He was returning to his position as head of the drama department for Goldsboro High School and needed an assistant. The job was Andy's if he wanted it, so the Griffiths made the move to 1208 E. Mulberry Street in Goldsboro, NC to start their lives together as husband and wife.

"While I was in college, I didn't have any notion of how I was going to become a professional entertainer," Andy once remarked. "All I knew was that I wanted to get up there and perform... then, when I wanted to get married, I realized I had no visible means of support, so I took a job as (a) music teacher... in the eastern part of North Carolina."

As he struggled through his daily routine at the school as Britton's assistant, Barbara found work as the musical director for the local Methodist and Episcopal churches and together they made a simple, if economical, living. Barbara was careful with their limited funds and tried to keep her more impulsive better half on a budget.

Andy on his method of teaching:

"I'd been hired as assistant drama coach—they had a fine drama department—but I was also supposed to build up the music department. That first year I taught three classes of drama, one of speech and one in music. Toward the end of the year I went around to all the teachers and asked if I could speak to the freshman classes. They didn't know what I was going to say (and) what I said was, 'Look, you kids want to take a crip course, take music, take glee club. You can't fail. No tests. No catches. All you have to do is sing!' And, that following year, I had three classes of music and a Boys' Glee Club."

This scheme worked, until the following year when he started off a class teaching music theory and sent one boy scrambling out of class. Andy was right behind the young man, who just happened to be the best tenor in the entire school:

"I bribed him back. I had to have him. I told him he was making a big mistake, leaving just as I was planning to give him the lead in *The Mikado*. That shook him. 'Just sit there and pretend to listen,' I told him. So he sat and picked up a little in spite of himself."

Despite his efforts, Griffith later admitted he wasn't the best choral teacher in the world. Especially in a large room with nothing between 125 teenagers and himself except for a piano. He once said that teaching music was like "teaching two things at once: a foreign language and mathematics. It's a little bit of both. It's nothing you can touch, something you have to equate to, like a flow of air."

Adding to his woes were later classes in, of all things, phonetics. He taught at Goldsboro High for three years and later termed himself miserable and bored the entire time:

"I knew my subject, but I couldn't seem to pass on my knowledge. There were some gifted kids in my classes, and I felt they were entitled to the best possible instruction. Well, I didn't feel I was the best possible instructor."

Andy knew his talents were not in education and he lacked the urge to discipline unruly students. Frankly, at 23-years-old, teacher Andy was too close to their ages for them to take him seriously as a disciplinarian. Griffith was less of a teacher and more of a pal.

But he knew how to get their attention, waving his long arms and bellowing out names and jumping up and down. Sometimes, he'd bring both fists down on top of the piano with a resounding crash to draw the room's eyes to him. And, after the room was silent, his face would split open into a wide smile and he'd take command... at least for a few moments.

His students liked him. They quickly got into the habit of calling the new teacher by a less formal name than "Mr. Griffith." To Andy's bunch, he was "Sport," because early on he'd told a hurried pupil who'd brushed by him to "Watch it, Sport," and the kids picked up on the phrase.

During the early spring of his third year of teaching in 1952, Andy and Barbara were studying voice with a teacher named Katherine Warren. At one of the lessons, a publicity man who was a friend of Warren's stopped to see her on his way to New York. Liking what he heard from the young couple Warren was working with, he offered the Griffiths a free ride and said he would set up an audition for them at the famed Paper Mill Playhouse in Millburn, New Jersey.

Aware of the Playhouse's reputation for staging high-profile summer musicals, Andy and Barbara jumped at the chance. However, upon arriving at the open auditions, they found the competition to be fierce.

"We lined up with over two hundred other people. Barbara sang 'In The Still Of The Night' and I sang 'Dancing In The Dark.' We were turned down. Someone standing around there told me my voice was overly brilliant—almost unpleasantly so. I didn't mind so much. In my own heart, I believed it. So, I decided to quit singing and start telling jokes," Andy remembered.

Then, Ainslie Pryor and his wife arrived in New York to meet the Griffiths and show them around the city. Their auditions fruitless, Andy and Barbara decided to accompany the Pryors back home. On the long train ride back Andy asked his friend (who was now also the director of the Raleigh Little Theatre) for a favor. He knew Ainslie was about to produce *The Drunkard*.

"I asked him if I could do a single performance between the play acts. I guess I figured if I couldn't sing, maybe I could talk," Andy said, and he auditioned for Pryor with his tried and true, foot-stomping, crowd-pleasing "Preacher Act."

By this time, the routine had grown in scope. Andy had continued to assemble the act from various sources, and it now consisted of a procession, announcements (no longer off-color), a sermon, the story of "The Preacher And The Bear," the closing hymn of "In The Pines" and a recessional.

Presented to the waiting Raleigh audience as "The Deacon Andy Griffith," the actor was an instant hit with his brash sermonizing.

Andy got the job, proving Pryor's faith in him... and reawakening his faith in himself: "That's when I realized there was a kind of acting, and a kind of writing, I could do, and maybe do it better than some other people could. I'd found my way."

Hence, came the full-blown creation of Andy's comedy monologues. Not content just to spout a series of one-liners and jokes, Andy instead became a master storyteller. He was in a state of constant creativity. Not having to worry about singing had freed him from any lingering performing inhibitions.

"Singing was always hard for me. It was a regimentation," Andy later said. "Standing up in front of an audience and talking was not hard for me, it was easy."

After telling his yarns repeatedly during his on-stage engagement at the Raleigh Little Theatre and having the routines received so well, Andy was all for rushing off to Miami to play the night clubs.

Sensibly, Barbara restrained him with the suggestion they play the "Rotary Club Circuit" instead—a market overlooked by many entertainers. Andy agreed, and started writing more material—perfecting his act with both new comedy monologues and rural versions of the classics.

"You can't rightly say I wrote 'em," Andy once drawled. "I'd just talk (my way) through the parts and Barbara would tell me if they (were) funny."

Later, when looking back at his early comedy days, Andy said: "I don't know how or where the ideas came from—I don't know why they came. But the notion to do (the) monologues came to me."

Years later, during his recording heyday in the late 1950s, Griffith shared credit for his success with Ainslie Pryor for giving him that much needed spot at the Raleigh Little Theatre. In the liner notes for *Andy Griffith Shouts The Blues And Old Timey Songs*, Andy wrote these words:

"Ainslie Pryor introduced the blues to me, or me to the blues, whichever is right, and helped me in the beginning in whatever career I've got more than anybody else. He helped me in many ways, including writing. He helped me write a lot of jokes and monologues I used to do—'Romeo and Juliet,' 'Swan Lake,' 'Make Yourself Comfortable,' etc. He was a brilliant man and his passing was a great loss to his friends and to the entertainment industry."

Andy and Barbara decided to become a performing duo, and worked up an act that featured singing, dancing, guitar playing and Andy's monologues. Larry Stith, a piano player, songwriter and singer was also part of the troupe and the group planned to tour the Carolinas presenting their act to any small venue willing to book them. They would serve as their own agent, handling the booking and the secretarial work so all of the money earned would come directly to them.

That fall, Andy took out $300 in teacher's retirement pay that had accumulated, accepted an offered loan for $750 from Robert Smith and another $250 from Jim Yokley (both old friends from Mount Airy), and bought a used Ford Station Wagon for the upcoming long distance travel.

Andy took the business venture, and the money borrowed to start it, very seriously. He knew this could be a one-time opportunity, and strived to make sure his benefactors knew of his dedication. The morals of his parents were ingrained deeply into Andy. Carl Lee Griffith didn't like being in debt, and neither did his son.

"I can never tell you how much I appreciate the offer of the loan you made me," he wrote to Robert Smith in the summer of 1952. "As I said when I saw you, the only insurance I can give you that it will be paid back is my word. I will make it good, even if the business should fail. In that event, I would take another job until I repaid my obligation to you."

Saying their good-byes to Goldsboro, Andy and Barbara moved to Chapel Hill, where they rented an unheated house far enough away from town to make rehearsals with their $10 upright piano possible without upsetting neighbors. Then, with a base of operations established, Andy and Barbara sat down and crafted a publicity brochure about themselves, describing their song and comedy act and where they could be reached for bookings.

"Unique Entertainment For Your Group With Andy And Barbara Griffith" the tri-folded promotional leaflet proclaimed. "No Occasion Too Small... No Job Too Big."

Inside was a series of photos of the couple performing and singing (including shots of Andy with the beard he sported during his last summer portrayal of Sir Walter Raleigh) and a brief biography and credits, which, while limited, did list their starring roles in *The Lost Colony*.

"Singing... Comedy Character Sketches... Interpretive Dances... Dramatic Readings... Vaudeville... An Ideal Program For Every Group And Budget," the brochure claimed. During these early performances, Andy was compared to Will Rogers. By this time, his rural resume of characters included "The Country Drummer," "The Guest Lecturer" and his soon-to-be famous "The Backwoods Deacon."

Barbara's singing and dancing abilities were also promoted heavily, listing her "lovely, dramatic soprano voice... in a wide selection including light opera, folk ballad and popular (music)."

After 500 copies of the leaflet were printed, they obtained lists from civic organizations across the entire state for any and all upcoming conventions and dinners for the next six months, hoping maybe one out of a hundred might have need of entertainment. Conventions, night clubs, clambakes... the Griffiths were willing and able to play them all and entertained civic groups from Rotary to Lions to Kiwanis.

And slowly, surely... the job offers started to trickle in.

"Those times were great, wonderful," Andy recalled in 1983. "It was a time of discovery for me. The discovery was the discovery of a kind of talent that I never knew I had and a kind of drive that I never knew I had. My energies were just right; they were razor sharp, and I was hungry. And I was writing things. I'd never written before. It turned out to be, I guess, a psychological thing. I was not a very good student in school. So these things (I wrote) are all based, in a way, on making fun of things I was afraid of."

Their first professional appearance was before the Asheboro Rotary Club in late October, 1952. The take was $75. Fifteen went to Larry Stith. Sixty went to Andy and Barbara for a night's performance. Small beginnings for the money and fame Andy was soon to claim, but not bad for a man who didn't enter the world of show business professionally until age 26.

"We had hard times," Barbara Griffith later said of those early performing days. "We've gone hungry, but we were never destitute. Something always happened to help us.... We didn't worry when we gave up the security of teaching and that weekly paycheck. We just knew we could make out all right.... When we didn't have money, we always felt rich. Our aspirations were bigger than making money.... And we had faith. We had faith in each other!"

In a single month, by November, 1952, the bookings were beginning to come in quicker than either of the Griffiths could have hoped. In a personal letter addressed to Robert Smith, Andy wrote of how quickly things were changing:

"We are moving along with the business very well. As a matter of fact, it is much faster than I expected it to be. We have two jobs in Mount Airy so far—Rotary in November and Kiwanis in December. We went to Asheboro about three weeks ago and did a show.... They liked it so well that they want us back for their ladies night."

"Barbara sang Puccini arias and popular standards," Andy said about those months spent driving back and forth across North Carolina. "I played the guitar while she did interpretive dances. And I delivered a monologue I'd made up called 'What It Was, Was Football.' "

During these performances Andy refined the now classic com-

edy routine that would make him famous and open the door t
television, Broadway and movies. "What It Was, Was Football"
featured his southern Deacon's drawled impression of his first grid-
iron game and soon became a requested Griffith staple.

The origins of "Football" are cloudy. Andy says he created the
routine on a hectic ride to a performance... and still has never gotten
around to writing it down on paper. The many things that went into
"Football's" genesis included his bemusement at his own lack of
skill in athletics... and a dirty joke about football told to Andy by
Vic Huggins, a Chapel Hill hardware store owner. "It was one of
those awful jokes that you never forget—only I never told it, ever,"
Andy stated.

"Barbara and I drove all over the state from one engagement to
the next, and it was on the road between Chapel Hill and Raleigh
that something happened that eventually took me away from North
Carolina," Griffith recalled about "Football's" creation. "I was thinking about a football game we had seen. It kept going over in my
mind and finally came out as a monologue which was called 'What
It Was, Was Football,' which had this country boy from the South
explaining what it was like watching his first football game."

Actually, Andy had seen many college football games in the
two years he played sousaphone with the university band. Always a
keen observer, he would watch the players... and he would watch
the fans. He saw them drunk and unruly, and endured having drinks
poured into his sousaphone. These observations, along with the
dirty joke, were churning in his mind on that fateful ride to Raleigh.... because Andy desperately needed new material. For the
first time in his career, he had been booked twice before the same
audience.

So, that night, he nervously presented "What It Was, Was Football" for the first time... and was taken aback at the applause and the
roar of laughter from the audience. Some clubs and organizations
grew to like "Football" so much, they invited the act back a second
time to hear it again:

"These people got so awful good at boring each other at these here conventions that any kind of entertainment looked good to them."

Griffith performed this specialty at the September, 1953 Greensboro, North Carolina convention of the Jefferson Standard Life Insurance Company, where it was put on tape for a mere $20. Orville Campbell, a Griffith fan who had previously heard the routine in (depending on which version you believe) either a Chapel Hill night club or at the Southern Short Course in Photography Convention in Charlotte, NC, was the instigator.

Campbell, the owner of a small recording studio in Chapel Hill, had presented Andy with a deal. By letting him record the monologue and releasing it on his Colonial label, Orville would split the profits 50-50. Griffith agreed, and soon after the independent record company pressed and released 500 copies of the routine on November 14, 1953. The bit (with Andy's rendition of "Romeo And Juliet" on the flip side) became an immediate local disk jockey favorite.

According to Griffith, he didn't think the record would sell, and in fact, the applause that comes up at the end of the "Football" routine was actually spliced on from Andy's rendition of "Romeo And Juliet" at the same convention.

Capitol Records became interested when their sales manager Hal Cooke noticed how well the regionally released recording was doing. Cooke knew other record companies were interested, so he sent out a representative from New York City to look into buying the master tapes.

Enter Richard O. Linke, a country boy by way of New Jersey who soon arrived in North Carolina to speak with Griffith and Campbell. When Linke walked into the room, Andy was suspicious of the fast-talking, well-dressed "city slicker." "His teeth are too close together," Andy whispered to Orville, eyeballing Linke with mock suspicion.

36

Linke later commented that Andy saw him as being "like a Hollywood gangster, like Cagney... Andy still thinks I was born at Forty-second and Broadway."

However, gangster or not, Andy stood his ground, and instead of the easy deal Linke had hoped for, Andy and Orville held out for either $5,000 or $10,000 (the exact amount is now hazy with time) and a cut of the profits... as well as a salary for Andy.

Taken aback by Andy's audacity, but impressed despite himself, Linke walked away after hours of dickering with the "Football" tapes, a $300 a week salary to assure Andy's recording exclusivity to Capitol Records... and a personal management contract for his new client. Soon after, Linke left Capitol and devoted himself completely to being Andy's personal manager.

"I dealt with a lot of record personalities," Linke said in 1960. "But I just had a feeling that this Griffith kid had a lot more on the ball than most. Fortunately, I was right."

Within weeks, Capitol had pressed and shipped the single... and credited the release to one Deacon Andy Griffith. An instant classic, the routine went on to sell over a million copies, and has been constantly re-released over the years—both as a single and on an array of comedy compilations.

With money now coming in, Andy and Barbara were able to settle their debts. In a letter dated December 12, 1953, Andy wrote his friend and benefactor Robert Smith with the news:

"Enclosed please find my check for the remainder of my loan and interest to date—how about that. This record is doing great things for us—Capitol Records bought it this week. The vice-president (Linke) no less flew down from New York to do it. He is also going to fix me up with TV and night club appearances. I swear I'm the luckiest person on earth.

"I have, of course, had disappointments but the complete picture has always been bright for me. Help has always been there when I needed it. And I want you to know that I shall always remember what you have done in making entertaining possible for me. I know you took a risk in loaning the $750 because there were a thousand things against any success we might have.

"Many people advised against going into it. But I guess always with prayer, faith and bullheadedness, it is always possible to have some degree of success."

After Christmas, the Griffiths left Chapel Hill. They moved into an apartment in Kew Gardens in Queens, New York while Andy's new manager went to work to make 1954 the year of Andy.

Barbara was happy for her husband, but at the same time it became apparent that Andy was now considered a solo act. When questioned about what Barbara would do next, Andy told reporters:

"... All (Barbara) wanted to do was get me started. Actually she wants to get going as an actress, but she'll have to lose her Southern accent. That's more than I'll have to do. I'll have to work at keeping it."

Linke had used his connections to secure Andy a contract with the famed William Morris Agency. Reportedly, the top brass at William Morris were so impressed with the young comedian that they took a hand in guiding his fledgling career personally.

First off in 1954 was a January spot for Griffith on *The Ed Sullivan Show*, which was then referred to by the same name as Sullivan's New York City newspaper column "Toast Of The Town." Sullivan was so excited about the North Carolina visitor's comedy recording that he wanted to book Andy for an unprecedented 18 appearances.

William Morris played it cool and told Sullivan that Griffith was only available for four bookings... they could discuss further slots down the line.

Unfortunately, Andy's nervousness and inexperience (this was his first exposure on television, and it was a live appearance to boot) resulted in a poorly received performance of the usual crowd-pleasing "Football" routine. When he walked off the stage, Andy would have no recollection of doing the monologue.

"After my first appearance, (Sullivan) called and wanted out of the next three! I never got a single laugh. I wasn't ready... in the old days if you played where you should play—for people in the front row—the people in the balcony (at that theatre) couldn't see you. So they would yell at you!" Griffith recalled in *The Official Andy*

Griffith Scrapbook. "The comic would have to stand maybe twenty feet back from the front row, which makes it tough! I just died that night, I absolutely died! I can still go in that theatre now and get an upset stomach!"

After his less-than-stellar spot on *Toast Of The Town*, Andy had an engagement at the famed Blue Angel. The posh NYC supper club was considered to be a top-notch room and the audience was filled with friends and supporters who wanted to see him succeed.

"I had friends in the audience the first night, and I scored heavy. And I had a man named Abe Lasko in the audience, he was the head of William Morris at that time. Abe is passed away now," Griffith remembered in 1993. "But he was a legend in his own time. And as he left that night, he said, 'Now I want you to go anywhere you can and learn how to entertain.' And I didn't have any idea what he meant until the next night. The next night I didn't have any friends in the audience. And I died."

With Lasko's words ringing through his mind every night of the torturous Blue Angel engagement, Andy soon discovered how hard it was to play before a night club audience:

"In a night club, people are eating and talking and moving around. To control them and command them to pay attention to you and enjoy it is the hardest job in the world... I learned a very important lesson from that experience, and that was how to draw and hold your audience, and that a person with something to say has to get the attention to be heard saying what he has to say. After that, I continued with my own monologues and put songs back into my act and went out on the road.... I learned to entertain.... "

Under the management of Linke, who took Lasko's advice, the young comedian was moved into the Southern night club circuit. Show after show, night after night, audience after audience. Andy played in towns like Tampa, Florida; Biloxi, Mississippi; Mobile, Alabama; Columbia, South Carolina and Fort Worth, Texas.

"Unlike my fellow colleagues around me in the business, I saw something else in a guy who was supposedly doing a country, or what you might call a rube act, you know?" said Richard Linke about his early days with his most famous client. "I once told someone in New York, I said, 'I got news for you. Andy Griffith is the hippest hillbilly you've ever met.' You bet your ass."

A year and a half later after being on the road, the actor was making $1500 a week and his confidence had blossomed. He learned how to handle an audience. "That's where I learned my trade," Griffith has said. "That Southern circuit is as tough a circuit as there is in the country. You either learned your trade or it'd kill you."

Of course, there were still misfires. One night, Andy found himself billed with a striptease act. "9! Beautiful Girls! 9!" read the marquee about his name. Andy groaned, and went to the management of the club to try and explain why he couldn't perform. By this time, Andy had acquired a rather large following of fans, many of which were high school age or younger... and the embarrassed Griffith said his conscience wouldn't and couldn't permit him to play an adult night club.

Then there was the time he was booked as an opening act for Mae West. Seems Andy was so amusing, audiences found West's act of innuendo and risqué tease a wee bit... anticlimactic:

"Her manager told me after the first show not to do that act again. So, in the second show, I did a different one, and the audience just went crazy. I was singing this song called 'In The Pines' and doing the preacher thing and stomping my foot, and they just loved it."

West herself had to admit that Andy's act was pretty funny.

Too funny.

Exit Andy as an opening act.

Then, while Andy was still touring around the country, Ainslie Pryor sent him a copy of Mac Hyman's best selling novel *No Time For Sergeants*. At the same time, another of Andy's old friends from his college days, R.G. Armstrong, called the comic raving about the book.

Finally, in Denver, Andy sat down and read the story of a country bumpkin draftee's encounters with the top brass of the United States Air Force. The more he read, the more excited he became. Andy knew this material was tailor-made for his talents. Perhaps another comedy record was ready to be born.

However, after Andy's representatives at the William Morris Agency checked into the rights for the book, they found the material had already been sold.

Disappointed, but still interested in the book, Andy slipped into his best southern accent and phoned Hyman, pretending to be one of the author's old high school buddies and drawling, "I wanna do a monologue on your book." The result of this friendly prank steered Griffith to Hyman's agent, a man named James Brown.

Reportedly, Brown's secretary was so impressed with Griffith she announced Andy to her boss with the words, "Mr. Brown, Will Stockdale is here to see you." Brown told Andy the rights were not available, but there were plans to make the book into a television show, a stage play, and hopefully, a motion picture.

Andy wasted no time in going to audition for the role of Will Stockdale, which was going to be dramatized by the Theatre Guild for the *U.S. Steel Hour* on the ABC television network.

"Here was this hillbilly and all," Griffith explained. "And I figured that if I couldn't play the part, well then, maybe I'd better try me another business. I mean, I was getting pretty well fed up with night clubs by that time, I'll guaran-damn-tee you!"

Unfortunately, the interview and audition with the Guild representative, James Haggerty, went flat. Griffith is more blunt in recalling how things went. "I had no technique, I was not an actor, I knew I'd flubbed it," he once said.

A dejected Andy walked back into the waiting room knowing he had to get another chance. He explained to the producers that he was never very good at cold readings ("I'm a talker, not a reader."), and despite their lukewarm response to his excuses and lack of enthusiasm about his chances, Griffith wasn't about to give up. He went outside and decided to wait, hoping to try again.

Then, fate stepped in. Andy told what happened next in an interview for *Carolina Lifestyle* in 1983:

"There was a lady sitting in the waiting room, had a fur coat draped over her chair. Don't know who she was, had no idea. She heard me talking, and at that time I had a heavy accent. She asked me what I did and I told her I worked night clubs, and she wanted to know if I sang and I said I talked. That fascinated her.

"She wanted to know what I talked about and I said Shakespeare, Romeo and Juliet, Hamlet. That fascinated her. Ballet, opera. That fascinated the hell out of her with my accent. '*Hamlet*?' she says. 'Do you do it?' I said no, I tell the story of Hamlet. She said, 'Well, do a little bit of it for me.'

"I was embarrassed... but I did it. As I started it, I realized something was happening. Gradually that room filled up. I got to a certain point and stopped and said, 'And it goes on.' They made me finish it, so I did the whole monologue. And that's how I got that job. I never would have gotten that part otherwise, never in a million years, because I didn't know how to read."

43

Griffith had been overheard by the right people, and at the conclusion of the piece, Haggerty called him back inside the studio with the news that he'd been hired. Alex Segal, director of the broadcast, shook his head in dismay at the young actor's inexperience, but saw Andy's potential in the role and agreed to take a chance.

According to writer Ira Levin, who wrote the teleplay from Hyman's novel, Griffith was electrifying in the part. "Some of the executives," Levin said. "Felt in rehearsals that Andy's performance in the show was so funny that they wanted to have an audience in there for a live reaction rather than use (the standard) canned laughter or added sounds... so the laughter on the soundtrack is authentic."

The first presentation of *Sergeants* was before a live audience of 150 people, and a television viewing audience of hundreds of thousands. One of these viewers was Maurice Evans, who was getting ready to produce the play on Broadway. One look at Andy as Will Stockdale and Evans knew he'd found his leading man.

On October 20, 1955, Griffith was the only transplant from the television production to open on Broadway in the play version of *No Time For Sergeants*, again with a script by Ira Levin and the show was a smash. The show was produced at the Alvin Theatre and greeted as a comedy sensation. Rave reviews made him a star overnight, with both the public and his fellow actors.

The October 31 edition of *Newsweek* noted in a review of the play that "All in one delightful stride, a thespian-nobody stepped into full stardom on Broadway last week... A swift series of oral and situational gags achieves, time after time, a show-stopping hilarity... held together by Andy Griffith's Pvt. Will Stockdale."

However, even if the on-stage Andy was smiling and self-assured that first night, inside he was as nervous as he had ever

44

been in his life. After the show's run in 1957, Griffith's
Roddy McDowall remembered Griffith's Broadway debut this w.

"The half hour before the curtain went up must have been the
worst in Andy's whole life. I've never seen a man so frightened.
We'd played New Haven and Boston and everything was fine. We
were pretty sure we had a hit. And all of a sudden, here's our star,
the one guy who can make or break us, standing on-stage frozen
stiff with fear.

"Luckily, the audience took to him right away—I don't know
what might have happened otherwise. A couple of people giggled,
then they began to applaud. Watching from the wings, you could
see old Andy's confidence coming back.

"He played Stockdale—right to the people. And they loved it.
He'd spot a lady in the second row all doubled up with laughter,
and he'd laugh right with her. That boy's quite a performer."

Myron McCormick, Andy, Roddy McDowall in
No Time For Sergeants

"You know what happened opening night?" Andy told an interviewer after that first performance of *Sergeants* was over. "They got on me, the other fellas, that I had to go over to this here Sardi's (restaurant) after the curtain, said it was a custom. Well, I didn't know nothing about that, but I went over with them. And soon as I walked in the door, darned if everybody in the place didn't stand up and start clapping for me. A man doesn't forget those kinds of things."

Later, Andy remarked: "You get this here feeling in the theatre—the people are right out there where you can see them. You say something funny and you hear them laugh... No matter what happens, I'll never get over the charge I got out of doing *Sergeants* on Broadway."

However, this charge came at a price. Don Knotts, who had a small role in the play and had befriended Griffith, once recalled trying to console Andy late in the run of the show after one performance just wasn't clicking with the audience.

"You can't do it every time," Knotts said with a shrug. Andy responded by spinning around and crying out, "Well, you can damn well **try**." To Griffith, if the audience wasn't spellbound, the show was a failure... and if the show was a failure, he was a failure.

After nearly 30 years had passed, Andy commented that he drew on his religious upbringing to "play Will as the most Christian human imaginable. All of the comedy came from that. It wasn't so much that the character was corn pone, it was that he was so honest and dedicated to doing right that it clashed constantly with the new society he was thrust into.... Will Stockdale, he only wanted to give. Will Stockdale never wanted to take—he never wanted anything for himself and he didn't care what anybody did to him. He might be hurt, but he would walk away from it."

Andy stayed with *Sergeants* for most of the entire run, leaving only after Elia Kazan offered him the role of megalomaniac Lonesome Rhodes in his satiric drama about the power of television, *A Face In The Crowd*—a film slated to be the biggest studio production ever shot in New York City.

Both Kazan and writer Budd Schulberg were coming off their pairing on Brando's *On The Waterfront*, and Griffith was excited to be considered for the starring role in their next big feature, which was based on Schulberg's short story "Your Arkansas Traveler."

Andy read the story, and a part of him responded to the character of Lonesome Rhodes. This was a role he knew he could play. He understood Rhodes, and thought he could become the character.

A first meeting with Schulberg proved unsuccessful. He still didn't see Andy as his leading man, despite Kazan's belief in the young actor. The writer agreed that "Griffith could give us the hillbilly stuff all right, but what about the power madness that dominates the whole second half of the picture?"

Griffith was determined to prove himself: "I wanted that part and Kazan thought I could do it, so he arranged another meeting with Schulberg—and that time I talked and acted just like Lonesome Rhodes, a guy who made you mad. The first time I'd been Andy Griffith, or Will Stockdale in *Sergeants*, who made you laugh."

A second meeting at Gallagher's in New York City went well, and Andy played to his instincts when he took the director and writer into a back room of the restaurant:

"(I) asked them if they had ever heard the famous evangelist Oral Roberts, as a healer. I then took Elia Kazan's head in my hands and *healed* him. I got that part, too... not getting it would have been a failure and would have gone against everything I believe in doing when the ball is handed to you."

"Andy seemed pretty one-dimensional with his quaint back-woods expressions and wide-eyed innocence. But we sensed another sort of talent underneath—an untapped strength, a wolf-in-sheep's-clothing kind of thing," a convinced Budd Schulberg later said.

"What made you choose Griffith for this part?" Kazan was asked after the deal was announced. "Isn't that pretty offbeat casting, even for you?"

Kazan just smiled and said, "Just a hunch."

Actually, Griffith had been mentioned for the role of Lonesome Rhodes even before *No Time For Sergeants* had appeared on Broadway. R.G. "Bob" Armstrong was touring in Kazan's stage version of *Cat On A Hot Tin Roof* and overheard Kazan wondering where he was going to find his leading man for *A Face In The Crowd*.

"Easy," Armstrong told Kazan. "Andy Griffith could do it."

"Bring him around, I'd like to meet him," the director responded.

Armstrong knew what he was talking about. After all, this was the very same Bob Armstrong who sat down with Andy one lazy summer evening and told him the story of Hamlet. His ties to Griffith stretched back to plays in Chapel Hill and *The Lost Colony* in Manteo. Armstrong had seen Andy act in comedies, musicals and dramas. He knew his old friend would be eerily perfect for the part.

With Kazan's helpful prodding, Griffith tapped into his darker side and found parts of himself most people would be loathe to admit even existed, much less bring out onto a Hollywood sound stage. And Mr. Rhodes wasn't the type of role one could leave behind at the end of the day either. Griffith commented on this soon after the picture wrapped:

"I guess I sort of became this character during shooting. That's how it is with me: I can't just play-act a part; I have to *be* it. And more then once I'd come home still all wound up in the story and give Barbara a little dose of Lonesome Rhodes. And I'll clue you in. That was tough on Barbara because he ain't a very decent guy to have around the house."

Andy would walk into their apartment surly and withdrawn. He would give his wife the silent treatment and not speak a word. Other times, he would explode, yelling and smashing closet doors. "You play an egomaniac and paranoid all day and it's hard to turn it off by bedtime," Andy told a *New York Times* writer. "We went through a nightmare—a real, genuine nightmare, both of us."

But years afterward, Andy would write of the experience as being worth all of the pain: "Making that movie was three months out of my life I wouldn't swap for anything. That was the first time I was called upon to play a serious dramatic part... I learned all I know about acting in making that one movie with Kazan... He taught me how to relate anything I had ever heard or ever read to what I was doing at the moment for the movie.

"I'd go over and tell him, 'I had an experience once.' And he'd say, 'Yeah, tell me.' Then, he'd listen and say, 'Yeah, that's right, that's right.' And I'd transfer that thought to what I was doing. Since my experience in that movie, I've tried to do everything I could to make myself feel any part I was playing.... "

Kazan would get Andy to reveal personal information—bits and pieces of his life that the director would then throw up against his actor to invoke a reaction. He believed these "chinks" in Griffith's psyche were the keys to finding the mix of anger, arrogance and self-doubt that made up Lonesome Rhodes, and with Andy's blessing Kazan would try and goad him with taunts.

Kazan thought he had found a good one in painting a picture of a miserable "Mr. Griffith" stuck in Goldsboro teaching high school

for the rest of his life, but Andy replied "That doesn't bother me....
I'll tell you some things that do."

Andy's worries of being mocked as a non-intellectual were
revealed. This, along with his fears of becoming an outcast in any
sort of discussion of literature or art were fodder for Kazan. One
morning the director instructed several members of the cast to
mock Andy for his ignorance—real or imagined.

Another whispered comment to Kazan about being called "white
trash" by a little girl he had a crush on during his grammar school
days was brought up by Andy, and how he saw the insult as meaning rejection. From then on, at strategic moments Kazan would
come up to Andy on the set and merely whisper the two words.

But Andy also had his own acting devices. A climactic scene of
Rhodes raving and ranting against the world from the balcony of
his New York penthouse was brought to life by Griffith before the
cameras even rolled:

"When they shot that speech, I told them, 'Bring me some
chairs, any old chairs around.' And I stomped them to pieces. It was
pathetic. For a few minutes... I didn't even know it was me—trying
to be this man.... It was a terrible thing, but this time there was a
reason... (but) it frightened me far enough so I'll never do it again.
For one thing, there's Barbara. For another, I don't believe in the
destruction of property. That's no way to live. It's bad, it's ugly and
it's black."

Andy's female lead, Patricia Neal, had no hesitations about
acting with the untried Griffith and understood the methods being
used to create Lonesome Rhodes. The real Andy Griffith was shy
around the other, more experienced members of the cast, but at the
same time he was soaking up everything. From day one he was
totally involved in the art of movie making. Neal once commented
that "Working with Andy was like working with family—I absolutely loved him."

The possibility of Griffith starting to put on any airs after starring in his first Hollywood motion picture was quickly put to rest on the last day of shooting. Andy emerged from the *Crowd* shooting sets at the old Biograph Studios in the Bronx wearing layer upon layer of suits—six suits to be exact, and he had topped off the half a dozen suits with a lush camel's hair coat.

"This here's my wardrobe," he explained. "They had all this stuff made up special for me. Cost over $900. I bought the whole works off of 'em for $300. You just know you can't beat that."

In 1957, Andy took time from his busy schedule to return to his hometown with Barbara to be honored on his birthday. The warm summer day was proclaimed as "Andy Griffith Day" and kicked off by a parade, after which the honoree received the key to the city at his birthday luncheon.

Andy was in good form, discussing his future movie goals ("I'd like to make a good Western sometime—something serious—like a Hopalong Cassidy maybe."), how often he cut his hair ("... mostly Barbara cuts it, only she usually has a small pair of scissors that are pretty dull... "), and where he got the ideas for his comedy monologues ("I guess I learnt most of my stories from my daddy. He had all kinds back then.... ").

In attendance were many of Andy's former teachers and friends. Sitting at the head table as Mayor W.F. Carter presented Griffith with Mount Airy's highest honor were the star's proud parents. No one was prouder then they were as Andy blew out the 31 candles on his birthday cake.

The following day, Andy and Barbara went their separate ways—she to Manteo and he back to New York for a round of interviews and further night club bookings. Andy took weeks before deciding how he felt about the accolades his former hometown had paid him, and he expressed this in a thank you note sent to Mayor Carter:

"I'm ashamed I've waited so long to thank you for the celebration you had for me in Mount Airy. I think the reason is that I just don't know how to thank you. I don't know that I have ever been so overcome by anything. I saw people that I haven't seen in years, and it's a real joy to know that Barbara and I have their concern and good wishes.

"For a while I wondered why you did all that, but then I realized you did it because you are proud and that makes us proud. We will try to live a life that will continue to make you feel that way."

Around this time, when asked if the records, the Broadway success and the film had made any difference in his life, Andy replied:

"Ain't no crowds knocked me down yet hunting my autograph. Once in a while somebody drives by to look at our place in Manteo, North Carolina, but that's about all. I just bought that house. It's on Roanoke Island—53 acres, trees, grass. Man, we've missed having a little open space around us, Barbara and me. Now, no matter what happens, we know that's home, the place we can really be free. We can fly to Hollywood or New York or wherever else I got to be, but Manteo, that's home."

The 53-acre farm also included a private dock and hunting preserve and was purchased by Andy for a then bargain price of $30,000.

In late 1957, Andy began shooting the film version of *Sergeants*, which was wisely left similar to the play in many respects. The film opened to solid reviews and rapid ticket sales, placing in the top five money makers of 1958. For the moment, between the dramatic range shown in *A Face In The Crowd* and the comedic skills (and dollar signs) of *No Time For Sergeants*, Andy Griffith was a sizzling Hollywood actor.

Hoping for another hit, producers tried to capture the magic again by casting Andy in *Onionhead*, which was released to theaters in the fall of 1958. The two projects shared many surface similarities, including military settings, a basis in a humorous bestselling book and Andy himself as the lovable bumbler.

Even the advertising campaign trumpeted "That Wonderful Guy From 'No Time For Sergeants' Is Goofin' Up The Coast Guard Now!"

They wish. *Onionhead*, despite a solid performance by its star, was a commercial and critical failure. Griffith was amusing and believable in the role of cook on a Coast Guard buoy tender during

Onionhead

World War II, but the comedy was ill-received by both fans and critics. Everyone generally liked the actor; they just didn't care much for the movie.

Griffith himself has dismissed the film, calling it "a real piece of junk."

"By that time I was kind of a name," Andy remembered. "I wasn't a name people would know all over the country, but I was enough of a name that I could get on any of the variety shows that they had. I could get on any of those and do my five to seven minutes."

However, the motion picture industry still primarily remembered him from *Onionhead*, and no new movie deals were being offered. Always ill at ease when not working, Andy decided to make himself available. He was doing well financially—much of the money he had earned had been invested in North Carolina businesses, including a supermarket, a record store, two music companies and various other pieces of real estate. But Andy was looking for something else.

"I had made my third picture, *Onionhead*, and it wasn't terrible good. In fact, it was terrible bad," Andy told *TV Guide*. "Well, we was sitting around with the William Morris (Agency) and I hadn't done a thing in that year. Not a blessed thing. And I asked them if there was any pictures coming up that I might do and they hawed around a bit and said, well, no, there wasn't. So I right out asked one of them, 'Has anybody asked for me?' And I guess this sort of caught him off guard because he said quicker than he meant to, 'No.' So I said, all right, let's see if we can get me a nice TV series."

Undaunted, Andy returned to the stage and assumed the lead in his first Broadway musical comedy *Destry Rides Again*, which opened at the Imperial Theatre in New York City on April 23, 1959. The sheriff's role had been played by a bevy of famous

54

leading men before Andy took the reins, including Tom Mix in 1932, James Stewart in 1939, Joel McCrea in 1950 and Audie Murphy in 1954.

However, Andy was the first performer to sing the part.

One reviewer noted of the Broadway production of *Destry* that "Andy Griffith plays the shy sheriff in easy style, singing surprisingly well." These words must have done Andy's heart good after earlier criticisms of his voice being "overly brilliant."

Destry Rides Again

Destry was well-received by audiences for the first three months, but soon entered into a slow decline that included deals where two tickets could be purchased for the price of one. Andy himself has always blamed the play's dramatic structure for bringing about an early demise: "The trouble was, the storytellers—the actors—were the lows between the highs—the dancers. Those dancers were great. That's the way the musical was written. And that's why it failed."

After flexing his vocal cords in *Destry*, both on-stage and for the original-cast album for Decca Records, Andy soon recorded another album for Capitol to follow up his first, *Just For Laughs*. This time, Andy wasn't laughing, and on *Andy Griffith Shouts Blues And Old Timey Songs*, he sang a wide variety of material.

At the same time, the busy actor was also doing as many television variety and talk shows as his schedule would allow, including hilarious spots for NBC's *The Tonight Show*.

According to Griffith, the Henry Hudson Theatre (where *The Tonight Show* was broadcast from) was "A wonderful comedy house. The audience was right on top of you."

When appearing on *The Steve Allen Show*, Allen would play to Andy's abilities to connect with an audience. The host allowed Griffith to be more intimate, bringing two stools out for Andy to present his monologues directly to the audience—and to the camera. Allen spent most of his time during Andy's comedic monologues laughing and falling off his stool. Allen's laughter was contagious and the audience ate it up.

In addition to television, movies, his records for Capitol and continual night club appearances, Andy was also being featured five times a week in his own CBS radio show—which was broadcast during the day before he would dress up to play cowboy at night.

Then, Richard Linke called. William Morris had a TV series proposal for Andy.

The Andy Griffith Show was born during a series of meetings held in Manhattan's elegant St. Moritz Hotel between Griffith, Linke and Sheldon Leonard. The first meeting was dominated by the gruff Leonard, who was riding high as producer of the hit *The Danny Thomas Show*.

A former actor, writer and director, Leonard had a concept in mind for Griffith. Along with writer Arthur (Artie) Standler, his idea was to place Andy as a small-town sheriff who also acted as the justice of the peace and the editor of the local newspaper. Andy would sit back, tell stories about his fellow townspeople and (hopefully) hilarity would ensue.

Then, Leonard hit his first obstacle. Andy wasn't sure this was such a great idea to hang a show on.

"(The sheriff) would have on his sheriff's uniform and as the justice of the peace he'd put on a black robe and as the editor of the paper he'd put one of those green visors on. It seemed kind of gimmicky to me," Griffith later said about his show's origins. "This character was not based on the character in *No Time For Sergeants*, but based on the history I'd had up to that point—a bucolic kind of sheriff. So I was supposed to be this funny guy who told funny stories about the people who lived in the town. And I could do it, but... I didn't care for the notion too much."

Leonard was both annoyed and intrigued by Griffith's attitude. He told Andy that "Ideas for shows are plentiful, but personalities are rare." Most actors would be doing handstands if given a chance to star in their own TV show, but as he soon learned, Andy Griffith was unlike any other actor Leonard would ever encounter.

Besides, according to Leonard, other people were interested in Andy. Bob Banner and Associates had also placed a bid for Griffith's talents. The television industry was hungry for new talent, and everyone could see the potential in a weekly show built around the popular actor.

Andy listened to Leonard's ideas and kept quiet, thinking to himself and nodding—and then, when the producer least expected it, Andy would ask detailed questions such as how the show was going to be financed and who the director would be. A stunned Leonard would look over at Linke in surprise. Where was Griffith coming up with all this? Linke would just smile.

In the fall of 1959, six hours of final discussions about the show were held, ending with a handshake agreement among the three parties. When the contracts were signed, Sheldon Leonard couldn't resist asking Andy about all of the waiting and talking before the deal was struck.

"Just wanted to know who I was dealing with," Griffith replied with a grin. "I never saw no sense in rushing things."

Actually, Andy was trying to decide whether or not to follow his own instincts. He liked Sheldon Leonard. He liked him a lot. If he signed on to do a television show with a man as talented as Leonard, Andy knew he would be in good hands. Quibbles over characterization could always be worked out as the show progressed.

But first, a pilot needed to be filmed. In January, 1960, Andy took two weeks off from *Destry Rides Again*. He was replaced by actor Hugh O'Brian in the lead role for two weeks while Andy flew to the Desilu Studios in Hollywood to film "Danny Meets Andy Griffith."

The pilot featured Andy as Sheriff Andy Taylor of Mayberry, Ronny Howard as Opie, and Francis Bavier as Henrietta Perkins, a local town widow. The characters of Aunt Bee and Barney Fife had not yet been created.

Mayberry's First Family

Andy brought his usual intensity to playing the folksy, smiling southern sheriff. When the cameras were on, his body relaxed and he presented the characterization of Andy Taylor beautifully. But when the cameras were off, he immediately went back to fretting— analyzing his performance, the script and whether or not he really wanted to subject himself to a weekly television series.

However, compared to the Danny Thomas method of working, Andy was as mellow and laid-back as Sheriff Taylor could ever hope to be. As Sheldon Leonard explained in *Inside Mayberry*:

"You have to realize, with Danny Thomas at the center, every-thing was conducted at a very high decibel level. Danny was not only loud, he was a screamer. So Andy, who's very quiet and laid back, is here in the middle of this group of screaming maniacs.... I went outside and met Andy out by the gate. I said, 'What's the problem?' Andy said, 'Look, Sheldon, I'm gonna do this series. I just can't do all that yelling and screaming.' So I said, 'Andy, it's not inherent in the (television) medium. Every show has its own personality. *We* adapt to *you*, and it will be built in a way so that you can live with it.' "

But even with Leonard's reassurances, the Thomas method made Andy nervous, and this in turn affected the early run-through of the pilot show. Andy said people were calling him "wooden," but as the show progressed he "got looser and looser and when they brought the audience in, I was on top of it.... "

The half hour comedy was shown as any other episode of *The Danny Thomas Show*, but Andy and company were the focus and viewers noticed. So did advertisers. "It was very flattering," Andy recalled. "The show was sold to sponsors that same night."

With the financial clout of General Foods backing the new show, there was no question of CBS clearing a spot in the upcom-ing Fall season. After completing his commitment to *Destry*, Andy immediately started work on the newly christened *The Andy Griffith*

Show. In less than three months, on Monday, October 3, 1960, the series premiered on CBS.

However, there was an important addition. Between the pilot and the upcoming first episode, Sheriff Andy Taylor acquired a deputy.

Enter Deputy Barney Fife, lover, fighter, policeman... and the man who Griffith has called "the finest comic actor I have ever known."

"Don Knotts was a friend of mine from a long time ago—he was on Broadway with me in *No Time For Sergeants*—and I didn't know he was at liberty," Griffith once said about the origins of Barney Fife. "He'd been doing *The Steve Allen Show*, and I didn't know he was free. Don called me and said he'd like to be on (my) show, and I said, 'Yes, call Dick Linke and Sheldon Leonard,' and he did."

Knotts was an ideal choice. He was born on a farm in the hills of West Virginia, but his father's health problems later resulted in a move to the city of Morgantown. Abandoning farming, the Knotts family ran a boardinghouse for students who attended the nearby University of West Virginia, but they never forgot their rural roots.

Unlike Andy, who had other ambitions as a child and teenager; Don was intent on being in show business from an early age. He had an older brother who was extremely funny and they would compete in a friendly way with each other. Don took great joy in being the class clown, picking up the nickname "Spider" because of his wiry build.

He was also a voracious movie watcher and loved radio. His idol was legendary comedian Jack Benny, and Knotts would spend hours trying to copy Benny's perfect comedic timing. He idolized

Edgar Bergen, teaching himself the art of ventriloquism. Throughout his high school days, the young actor would entertain civic groups with his own wooden dummy and an act he admits to "borrowing" from Bergen.

After high school, Knotts enrolled as a speech major at the University, with the intention of becoming a teacher, but his academic plans were interrupted when World War II broke out. Leaving his studies, Don joined the army. A wise superior officer realized the lightweight Knotts was not designed for combat and assigned him to Special Services, where Don spent the next two years touring the South Pacific doing comedy routines in a production called *Stars And Gripes.*

When he was discharged, his goal of becoming a teacher had changed. He returned to school, received his degree in speech... and took his diploma to New York City. His talents were soon on display in such radio and television programs as *Bobby Benson's B-Bar-B Ranch* and *Search For Tomorrow.*

Don also kept an eye on Broadway and was finally presented with his first stage work in *No Time For Sergeants* where he first met Andy and the pair developed their close friendship.

After *Sergeants,* Don began to appear regularly on *The Garry Moore Show* and *The Tonight Show.* Later, he hit his stride on Steve Allen's Sunday night show, where he was allowed to stretch his talents. When Allen took the show from New York to California, Knotts followed. By this time he had perfected a character he called the "Nervous Little Man" (based on an after dinner speaker observed back home in Morgantown) and had carved out his own niche...

Until *The Steve Allen Show* was canceled.

Then, after seeing the pilot for *The Andy Griffith Show*, he was inspired to call Andy and simply ask, "Don't you need a deputy?"

With Andy's approval, a part was created for Don and by the time the second episode of the show was filmed, it became apparent that the addition of Knotts as the high-strung Barney had altered the tone of the series. Knotts, Griffith and the show's writers were all involved in the final result.

"I was supposed to have been the comic, the funny one," Andy said. "(The show) might not have lasted even half a season that way, but when Don came on I realized... Don should be funny and I should play straight to him."

Even before the show premiered, Griffith already had formed his opinion of how the show would grow. "It won't be all comedy," he said. "And we'll be using lots of fine character actors. It's sort of easy to get too much of me."

With a television series now underway, Andy and Barbara had to move from Manteo (and New York City) to California. By this time their family had expanded with two adopted children: Sam, born in December, 1957, and Dixie Nann, born in September, 1959.

The Griffiths ended up buying a home in the San Fernando Valley at Toluca Lake, which, as Andy once termed it, was "just a mountain away from Hollywood." The home was in a nice, quiet neighborhood which is exactly what they were looking for... for their children and for Andy's own peace of mind.

Andy was to write in 1961: "When I was growing up in Mount Airy, NC, if anyone'd told me my wife and I would be owning a home in Toluca Lake ... and I'd be starring on a television show, I'd have thought they were plain silly. But that's the way it's been. We moved out here just a year ago... And we brought only our clothes with us. Nary a stick of furniture. We weren't sure but that we'd be going home in a few months."

Richard Linke also made the move, and was just as nervous as Andy. In New York, Linke knew everyone and had contacts galore, but in Los Angeles he needed time to establish himself. As part of the deal to sign Andy, Linke was made associate producer of the new show—to protect himself and his client.

While interiors for *The Andy Griffith Show* were filmed inside the Desilu Studios, the exteriors were shot at Forty Acres, a general designation for the back lot in Culver City, California. The area was a mish-mash of building fronts and sets, including a Mexican village, a portion of a bombed-out European city, a western street... and a downtown area of homes and shops better known as Mayberry. Television and movie buffs might recognize the town in earlier incarnations from either *Gone With The Wind* or *The Untouchables*.

"Funny thing about the Mayberry we know at Forty Acres," Griffith once said in an article titled "All About Mayberry," "Is that even though all of the buildings are false fronts, when you're working there you get the feeling of being in a small town. You forget that on the other side of the fence is one of the biggest cities in the world."

While picturesque, the Desilu back lot lacked certain amenities. There was only one telephone, no cafeterias or nearby restaurants, and the heat could be fierce. But it became home, and as he settled into place, Griffith realized he wanted to make Mayberry a real place. A place with texture and people and heart.

"(The) show was not set in North Carolina to start with. It was just somewhere in the south, but I hated saying things like Central City. I wanted to say Siler City, which is a real town," Andy remarked. "Finally, we started saying Siler City and Charlotte, Raleigh, Asheville and it just became North Carolina, and I think it helped."

As for the setting being too country, viewers didn't seem to mind, placing the show in the top five. Worried about overdoing his famous Southern drawl, which he can control to a marked degree depending on the character and the situation, Andy once said:

"I have found that there is a very thin line between the real and the phony when you use Southern accents... What most people don't realize is that there is a pleasure, a musical-like satisfaction, in using a definite Southern manner of speech. Southerners enjoy words, accenting them in a certain way. In England, the language is enjoyed much the same way."

Once the actor wondered aloud to Dick Linke about his accent. "Say, you think I ought to lose my southern accent?" he asked.

"Sure," Linke replied dryly, "If you want to try another line of work."

During the 1961 summer hiatus of the television show, Andy co-starred with Debbie Reynolds in the Twentieth Century Fox comedy-western film *The Second Time Around*.

Unfortunately, Andy had agreed to his role without mentioning he didn't know how to horseback ride. His lack of knowledge presented itself early during a scene where Andy was to ride up and greet a waiting Reynolds and Thelma Ritter.

The first take had Andy riding around a corner bouncing up and down in the saddle like "two hundred pounds of jelly wrapped in buck-suede" according to Reynolds' recollection in her autobiography. In addition, Andy was muttering a steady stream of epithets since he had neglected to wear an athletic supporter.

When Andy finally reached the girls, he brought the horse to a halt, prepared to dismount, lost his footing and slid hard off his mount to the ground.

The Second Time Around

The director suggested Andy go put on a jock strap and they would try again. After the pain of his first ride, Andy didn't disagree and returned fifteen minutes later for another go.

Take two: Upon stopping, Andy's foot slipped out of the stirrup and down he went to the ground for a second time.

Take three: A now mad Andy rode up and promptly slipped out of the stirrup and fell off the horse again.

Luckily for Andy (and the horse), the scene was captured perfectly in the fourth take.

After the end of filming at the movie's wrap party, Reynolds presented each member of the cast and crew with an individual present. For Andy, she'd raided the prop shop at Fox and absconded with a genuine stuffed Palomino.

"A little something you can practice on," Debbie chuckled as the horse was rolled up to the shocked Griffith. Delighted with the gift, Andy decided to take his new horse home with him that very night, but the only way he could transport it was to anchor it to the top of his station wagon.

Unfortunately, while driving home Andy was stopped by the California Highway Patrol. The officers wanted to know why Andy was driving around with a dead horse lashed to the roof of his car.

Andy responded with: "Listen, this horse here is my friend. Roy Rogers stuffed Trigger, so I stuffed this. It's my pet horse."

Since there was no law against stuffing a horse or driving around with one on top of your car, they let Andy go.

After returning to Desilu, Andy and Barbara traveled together on a coast-to-coast publicity tour for CBS to promote the upcoming second season of *The Andy Griffith Show*. At the end of the tour, Andy was questioned about why he thought his series had already worked its way into the top ten. His comments prove that the savvy actor had already put his finger on why the show worked so well:

"Our director, Bob Sweeney, calls our show a family show with a border of insanity about it. I'm mostly just the moderator throughout. I work most successfully that way. We get into trouble if the show revolves around *my* troubles—then we get the cutes. Don Knotts and I are actually a comedy team. I play straight man.... One thing we've talked about a lot is the way a comedian is born. Don says a comedian is born out of either unhappiness or embarrassment and at sometime in life, perhaps when you're about three or five years old, you start to learn to protect yourself. When you're laughed at, you turn it to your advantage."

"So now we're getting ready to start our second season on TV," Andy wrote before the new slate of shows premiered. "I'm right glad the people have accepted us. I like show business. Means I won't have to take a job in a furniture factory, like I always figured I would."

After winning an Emmy for Best Supporting Actor for the first year of his work as Barney Fife, it was obvious others were aware of the chemistry between the lean, hyper Knotts and the reassuring, folksy Griffith... and no one was more aware of this than Andy:

"I hate to see myself on the screen," Griffith mentioned to an interviewer while sitting for a photo shoot for *The Chicago Tribune*. "Except when I'm doing something with Don. We can almost feel one another breathe—that man is so good you just can't believe it. He is so intense, he looks at me so deeply, he's trying so hard that half the time I just bust up right there on the set and we have to start all over."

"We had similar backgrounds," Don Knotts once said. "We were both from rural areas and similar religious backgrounds. When we talked about our relatives, they all seemed to be the same. Our sense of humor clicked. And we had the same idea of timing."

After a year of redefining the character of Sheriff Taylor (less rube, more leading man) and finding he could contribute to the writing process of the series, Andy (if such a thing is possible), became even more focused. In a two-part article on the show, *TV Guide* was soon to refer to Griffith as being the "Cornball with the Steel-Trap Mind."

A hard worker and a hard worrier, Andy usually began his day at 5:30 in the morning reading his script and having cereal and coffee and would often arrive on the Desilu lot half an hour earlier than anyone else. He worked 16 hours a day, 39 weeks a year, to make sure the quality he insisted on was maintained.

"I was very protective of that show, you have to understand that," Andy later said. "I was watching everybody all the time. And, I never went up to another actor, unless I knew him really well, and criticized him or suggested that he do it another way. But I'd been in on these scripts from the outset.... So I had a notion, a preconceived notion as to how they should be done. I realize people say, 'Things can be done hundreds of different ways.' That's true. But if you have written it and you hear it a certain way and it doesn't come back that way, it'll drive you crazy after a while."

Andy had good reason to be protective of his show. He and Linke owned over 50 percent of it. The rest was divided between Sheldon Leonard, Danny Thomas and producer/writer Aaron Ruben, who had been brought on to oversee the day-to-day operation of the series. Linke and Griffith had borrowed heavily to ante up their share of production costs. However, since the show was an instant success, they were soon able to pay back their bank any borrowed sums.

"While Andy did not actually write a complete script, his comments and suggestions were invaluable," Aaron Ruben has stated regarding how the star involved himself with *The Andy Griffith Show*. "Andy would not leave the table where we would be doing a final re-write until he was satisfied that not just his lines were exactly right, but that of every other character in the script. I honestly don't know how successful the series would have been without his input and the authenticity he brought to it."

However, Griffith was always quick to credit the writers of the series: "I think our writers are nothing short of geniuses, the way they've caught the feeling of North Carolina without ever being there."

Even Don Knotts wasn't immune to involvement with rewrites: "Sometimes, if a bit that had come in from the writers didn't quite make it, we'd scrap it and (Andy would) set me in a corner and say,

'Here, write something.' " Eventually, Knotts would also attend script meetings and sit by Andy's side. The rest of the actors were allowed to give input into their characters as well, and the series became even stronger as a result.

During his time spent working on the show during the 1960s, Andy's home life was sedate enough... at least on the surface. If there were problems, Griffith's legendary concern for his own privacy, and the privacy of family, kept any marital discord behind closed doors.

For example, the stress of working on *The Andy Griffith Show* usually revealed itself in the form of Griffith's mercurial temper. Once, during the first season of the show in a fit of anger, Andy put his fist though a door at his home... suffering several broken bones. The cast he was forced to wear on the show was explained away as a fishing accident and the official word was that he injured his hand building a toy garage for his son, Sam.

However, thirty years later, in a 1990 *TV Guide* piece, Andy was to blame this incident (along with other blow-ups during the run of the *Griffith* show) on other things besides his own perfectionism and the grind of doing a weekly television series:

"You know, everybody says as you get older, you get calmer. Not true. Person just discovers some things are self-destructive... But I should tell you that when I broke my hand, it never had anything to do with my professional life.... "

When queried point-blank about personal problems, Andy repeated himself a second time with, "It never had anything to do with my professional life. You figure it out."

A telling scene of the pressures inside Griffith occurred in 1963, at a CBS television special where the stars had come out to plug their shows. At a lunch break, as Andy munched on a sandwich and brooded over his script, he was approached by the grand dame of television comedy, Lucille Ball.

"You play golf, Andy?"

Andy shook his head "no."

"You should. It would do you some good." Lucy paused, and added. "But, you don't do anything you don't do well, do you?"

Andy, Lucy and Danny Thomas cross swords in a CBS special

Later, in recalling the incident, Andy noted:

"It's true. Lucy knew what I've just found out about myself. All my life I've been thrown into situations I couldn't always master. Riding a horse, teaching school, getting adjusted to new places, new situations. It's a long way from North Carolina to Hollywood. And mostly, if I couldn't do something right, I'd quit to save myself embarrassment. It drives me crazy not to be able to do something well. And, I drive people around me crazy, trying too hard, being so intense. Sometimes, I like to give my wife fits with this rebellion I've got going on inside. The only good thing is, I think I'm gaining on myself."

In an interview with Barbara Griffith given around this time, she said in regards to Andy's already legendary work habits: "A comedian's wife has a hard job. It's a constant state of giving. A continual satisfying of the other's needs, because a comic is like a child. Everything must revolve around him."

Barbara quickly followed this up by noting Andy's devotion as a father and how he was "an extremely good family man who's kind and thoughtful about relatives, both his and mine... (even though) he frequently lives in a world so completely surrounded by himself that often he doesn't even hear me.

"A person who deals in himself and in his emotions is bound to be more sensitive than a butcher," Barbara added. "So we try to soft-pedal when Andy has had many tensions building. Otherwise, you can never tell when it's that last trivial thing which will be the straw that broke the camel's back."

After Andy learned of Barbara's comments from the very same interviewer, he was cagey, but still polite for his part of the interview, until asked "Does a big star like you ever have to guard against acting like a big man?"

"Any way I answer that, I've got to come off sounding like a big jerk," Andy replied with a hint of annoyance. "If I say, 'Yes, I sure do have to watch myself that I don't act like a big man,' I'm admitting I *am* one—which sounds as stupid as hell. If I say, 'No, I don't have to,' I'm setting myself up to be a very fine person. Either way, I'm in trouble.

Andy paused before continuing: "To give you a truthful answer, I can only say I don't find myself doing impossible things. If I'm mad at somebody, I go directly to that person and have it out right at the moment—and we eventually arrive at some conclusion.

"I'll give you a direct answer. And that is that I guess I am somewhat arrogant sometimes, sure. But so's everybody. And I do have a pretty violent temper. I sure do. Both at work and at home. Once I displayed it on-stage. But I try not to do that anymore. It disrupts work... As for acting like a big person at home, all I know is, when I want to sit down, I just go find me a chair and sit. Barbara doesn't carry one around waiting for me to snap my fingers. And she just fills up the coffee pot at night. If I want it, I go get it myself."

As for bringing stress home from work?

"I do have a pretty bad temper. At home, I distinctly remember one time when I had a real violent fit of it. I got so angry that I literally... and I mean actually... tore one of our doors down in a blinding rage. I eventually ended up apologizing. I bought my wife some flowers... and a new door.

"Guess maybe there's some difficulty in handling me—or anybody successful, for that matter. But there's less with us, because I married Barbara before I became a star... My wife saw the whole gradual process. As I started growing bigger and having larger problems, she grew right along with me."

72

By mid-1963, an estimated 36,000,000 people were watching the show, and Griffith was receiving more than 1,000 fan letters a month. However, even though the fans were there and the ratings kept the show's sponsors happy, Griffith was distressed by the view that Mayberry was populated by "hicks."

"Besides the comedy, we've got a lot of love and affection there in Mayberry. Folks in Mayberry are forever doing something for folks they think a lot of, know it? But we aren't sappy or mawkish. We have no truck with treacle. We aren't a bunch of hokey yokels, neither. It grieves me when they refer to us as a hillbilly show, which we aren't by any stretch."

Other well-heeled fans of the program also came to its defense. Famed television writer and creator of *The Twilight Zone* Rod Serling frequently drifted in from working on his own series to watch *The Andy Griffith Show* being filmed. Serling insisted the *Griffith* show was "one of the few genuinely funny comedies in the medium... What hits me is that the people are characters, not caricatures."

"There's a great chemistry between all the people on our show," Andy commented to an interviewer. "We all work well together, possibly because we're all friends. Not just friendly friends, but real close friends. I know we'll continue to be after the show goes off the air. When we get together we enjoy what we're doing whether it's playing or working and, if we enjoy it so much, it stands to reason that other people will too."

In the space of three seasons and nearly 100 episodes, a series of female leads for Andy had come and gone, including actresses Elinor Donahue, Julie Adams, Sue Ann Langdon and Joanna Moore. "That one almost caught fire," said Aaron Ruben in 1963, referring to Moore, "But Andy keeps saying, 'I don't want to have a show with fights in the kitchen.' "

"That whole first year (there was this) conventional notion that we had to get Andy a girlfriend—and Andy was very uncomfortable with the notion anyway to begin with because he didn't have the right approach to it by his own admission," Aaron Ruben later remembered in a 1990s interview featured in the book *America On The Rerun*.

"To this day, if you ask him, he says he doesn't like to look at those first year's shows, particularly the ones (dealing) with women because he was being a comic and an awkward one at that, in terms of these women... but once he arrived at (the) conclusion that he was now a leading man, he could be more comfortable with women. He could deal with them on a straight forward basis and not behave like some goofy teenager."

Good friends

According to show legend, the producers and writers had given up on finding widower Andy Taylor a steady girl, until Aneta Corsaut was hired as Miss Helen Crump, Opie's teacher. Corsaut's appearance was designed to be a one-shot, until mail started to come in. A second script was written for Miss Crump, and a third, and finally, she was signed to a contract. "When (Aneta) came in, it worked.... Aneta had a mature, adult approach," said Aaron Ruben.

"Andy was very shy with women.... I think just the fact that he was comfortable with me personally made it possible for the characters to develop," theorized Corsaut in *Mayberry, My Hometown*. "Also, I think it was because we got into a huge argument about women's rights the first day on the set. We were out in the middle of the street on location screaming at each other and it ended up being very funny to both of us and we became friends."

In the fall of 1964, Jim Nabors left *The Andy Griffith Show* to star in his own spin-off series, *Gomer Pyle U.S.M.C.* Gomer traveled cross-country from Mayberry to a Marine base in California, where his innocent manner and country common sense soon became the bane of his long-suffering superior, Sergeant Vince Carter.

In the premiere episode, Andy Taylor accompanied Gomer to his new show and hung around to make sure his friend would be able to cope in the new surroundings. Gomer had no problem, as Andy and *Gomer Pyle U.S.M.C.* series creator Aaron Ruben knew he wouldn't.

After all, a younger and much broader-acting Griffith had played Will Stockdale in three successful incarnations of *No Time For Sergeants*. Stockdale was in the Air Force and Gomer in the Marines, but other than being in different branches of the Armed Forces the two southern boys had lots in common.

Amusingly enough, during the same 1964-1965 television season, a *No Time For Sergeants* TV series, with Sammy Jackson in the Griffith signature role of Will Stockdale, was scheduled by ABC opposite *The Andy Griffith Show* at 8:30 on Monday nights. Obviously, viewers chose to stay with the real thing and also found room to follow their pal Gomer over to Friday nights.

By this time, *The Andy Griffith Show* had grown so much in popularity that CBS began broadcasting weekday reruns at 11:00 in the morning under the title of *Andy Of Mayberry*—a title chosen not only to help watchers tell the difference between the syndicated and the regular network broadcast version of the show, but also a sly comment on how the very town of Mayberry had become a character in its own right.

"The town of Mayberry is as much a character on the show as Sheriff Andy Taylor," Griffith once said. "That's by design, through the memories of all of us on the show. The dress is modern... but the mood and atmosphere are in the '30s. We keep the problems small and become concerned over them."

Another time, Andy noted: "So much of Mayberry is like it used to be. We drive 1963 cars and we dress modern and all the stories seem to be taking place at the present time, but there are overtones of a past era. It's this sense of nostalgia we create; it's this feeling that Mayberry is timeless."

Then, there are those who think Andy Taylor and Andy Griffith are interchangeable, and on the show Andy merely played himself, but the man himself was always the first to refute this:

"I wish I could be like Andy Taylor. He's nicer than I am—more outgoing and easygoing. I get awful mad awful easy... Andy Griffith and Andy Taylor are similar in some ways. In other ways, they're completely different. I'm not as good as Andy Taylor; he almost always tries to live his life so that he is responsible, and he realizes his responsibility—not only to his family, but to his friends, his girl and his community."

However, Griffith is also a compassionate and thoughtful man. The cast and crew of *The Andy Griffith Show* had been rocked when actor Howard McNear suffered a debilitating stroke in 1963 that put him in a coma for a short time. After awakening, McNear was unable to work while recovering, and the show was forced to go without his gentle characterization as Floyd Lawson, Mayberry barber supreme.

However, Andy had not forgotten McNear, and when the opportunity presented itself, he called the actor's wife to see if perhaps Floyd might be able to come back to the barber shop. Helen McNear told Andy "it would be a prayer answered." Howard's health and condition had greatly improved through physical therapy and his mind was as sharp as ever.

Andy knew McNear had limited mobility and little use of his left arm, so he made sure in scripts to have Floyd either seated or standing behind the barber chair using a hidden brace for support. Griffith's loyalty was repaid in having a key cast member return to the show, where McNear stayed until the seventh season and further complications of the stroke began to affect his speech.

McNear's son Kit has said:

"I don't think any other cast or individuals had the guts that Andy Griffith did. I think it is really unusual, virtually unheard of, for a production company to look after one of its members like that. But that's the way Andy wanted it. I really, really have to praise Andy Griffith. I will always respect and admire Andy Griffith for that."

Griffith has also always freely admitted to his tendency to keep his emotions bottled up inside:

"It's the way we mountain people are," he once tried to explain. "My own grandpappy never showed big emotion but once in his life. Lying on his deathbed, he suddenly got up and kissed my grandma gently on the cheek—he'd never been seen before even to touch her! Then, he took back to his bed and died. One emotional act in his whole life, but no one ever forgot it.

"I used to think, 'Oh, boy, (when) I finish the series and then we retire to Manteo.' Well, that's not the way it works. A man changes... he learns, he observes, he grows. I still love North Carolina with all I've got, but the truth is, I know now that Los Angeles is my home. A man has to live where he competes, and I know now that I'm going to have to work and compete in show business—it's the only thing I do well.... I always figured I'd get out as soon as I could, away from the pressures. Now, I can't run away. This is my life. And I guess I have to live with it."

Still, he loved his time off and enjoyed fishing and skeet-shooting and driving around in his camper with Barbara and the children. When at home in Manteo during the late spring he was at peace, knowing the locals respected his privacy. Everyone knew where Andy lived, but no one ever told the tourists.

In a 1965 radio interview with Fred Robbins on *Assignment Hollywood*, Andy commented on how success had altered his lifestyle. As usual, he downplayed the enormous changes—and pressures—he was now facing:

"Well, I very honestly can't say that much has happened (since my success). I'm very happy with my life, happy doing the show, happy living out here in Los Angeles. But I can't say that my life has changed any more than the fact that we're secure, and my wife Barbara goes ahead to the store and gets whatever she wants and brings it home; you know, we don't buy day-old bread anymore."

Before the original five-year *Andy Griffith Show* contract ended for the 1964-1965 season, Don Knotts had begun looking for another home since Andy had always said after five years the series would be over. "I interviewed with all the networks. I was very hot with that show, so I could have had almost anything I wanted," Knotts remembered.

Universal Studios presented Don with an opportunity to star in a series of motion pictures. He would have his own office, choice of writers and a five-year contract. Don felt free to accept Universal's generous offer that would go on to make him a top movie draw for the remainder of the 1960s.

Then came word that Andy was going to stay on with the show, and of course he wanted his deputy by his side. He came to Knotts with a generous offer, but it was too late for Don to get out of his commitment.

"Andy... maintained from the beginning that he was going to do five years and that was that," Knotts said when explaining his departure from the series. "He just felt that was long enough to stay on the air. So I started to look around and I got this offer from Universal. While we were negotiating, Andy changed his mind....

"He asked me if I wanted to stay, and I told him I had this good offer to help create and star in my own movies. I thought it would be a good move on my part. So he agreed and said, 'Why don't you go ahead then and whenever you have time, we'll write you in here and you can come back and do guest shots.' "

It was a generous gesture from Griffith. But he knew—everyone involved knew—the comic chemistry that drove the show was gone. The rhythms had changed. Even though *The Andy Griffith Show* would remain in the top ten, reaching the status as the number one show in the country during its final 1967-1968 season... the golden years, for the most part, were over.

There were still fine episodes, fine writing and fine performances... but a Mayberry without Barney Fife wasn't the same.

Andy commented on the Andy and Barney relationship in 1985:

"It's a relationship—I can't really explain it. It's a love relationship between two men. I don't mean sexually, but just—these two characters really cared for each other, and Andy was devoted to Barney. Andy would watch Barney do something that he knew was going to hurt him, and Andy would always be sure that he was there to catch him just before he hit the ground. The reason it worked so well I think is because Don and I were such good, close friends. He and I stayed together. We never did socialize very much in the evening, because we didn't need to. We had already spent about twelve hours with one another, talking or laughing or doing something or working on camera.

"Don left after the fifth year and I remember the last shot. Don was on camera and I was off camera.... We finished that show, and each Wednesday we would have a little party and we would have two or three bottles and some stuff to eat for the crew and anybody that wanted to be there... and after a while, I looked up and the stage was empty. They had all left very quietly. They recognized the friendship that (Don) and I had with one another and they allowed us that last moment together. And I said, 'They're gone. We might as well go too.' So we went out the door and he was parked over that way and I was parked over this way and he says, 'Well, call me sometime.' I said, 'Okay.' And we have for years and years."

The phone soon rang. October 7, 1965 brought an unusual prime-time variety special to CBS under the lengthy name of *The Andy Griffith, Don Knotts, Jim Nabors Special*. The hour-long color presentation was unusual in that much of the show had a distinct Mayberry flavor, even down to Andy and Don reprising their Sheriff Taylor and Deputy Fife roles in a sketch that told why Andy hired Barney to become his deputy.

80

Even more wacky was a musical number when the three actors proceeded to sing and dance in costume and in character as their Mayberry alter-egos. Andy Taylor, Barney Fife and Gomer Pyle make for an entertaining, if slightly surreal, trio.

The special's origins came about when Richard Linke set up an appearance for the trio in 1964 at a Lake Tahoe resort. This was a one-time booking, and he told the performers to relax, breathe the fresh air, and do what they did best.

Andy told a few monologues, Nabors sang, and Knotts became the "Nervous Little Man" once more. They also acted together in comedy sketches. The show was simple and straightforward and the Lake Tahoe audience loved it. Linke had the success of that night in mind when CBS came to him and inquired about putting some of his clients in a special.

"This is the last time we'll work together," Griffith said during the filming of the special. "We all have our other work to do—Jim with his series and Don at Universal.... It's tough to arrange our schedules so we can be together. But we're still friends. Matter of fact, that's the theme of the show, friendship."

"Friendship" was shown in songs and routines where the trio of performers were allowed to demonstrate their versatility with a full chorus, orchestra and dancers. Even more amazing, thanks to writer Aaron Ruben's involvement, everyone was in character. TV watchers were amazed to not only have Andy, but Barney and Gomer together again as well.

The special, Griffith's first, was so successful that CBS signed him to a three-year contract calling for one special a year.

The 1965-1966 season after Don Knotts's departure was a troubled one. A nephew of Floyd's, Warren Ferguson, was created as a replacement deputy. A stand-up comedian named Jack Burns was given the task of attempting to fill Don Knotts's place, and as might be expected, he was unable to meet the demands of the role.

"So we put (Jack) on—and we said we were not replacing Don—but we were replacing Don and we were giving him Don Knotts material—and it didn't work," Andy said in Richard Kelly's definitive history of *The Andy Griffith Show*. "I can't begin to explain how uncomfortable we were. I get strung out pretty easily, and if I'm uncomfortable I'm hell to be around, and I was *very* uncomfortable... It wasn't Jack's fault, it was our fault."

Knotts would return five times as Barney Fife, winning Emmy Awards twice for his guest appearances. Andy repaid the favor by helping in rewrite sessions for *The Ghost And Mr. Chicken*, Don's first film for Universal. According to Knotts:

"When I did my first movie... we incorporated an unseen character in the movie who yelled, 'Atta Boy, Luther' to me. Well, Andy came out to help us with a rewrite on that movie. We had gotten into some trouble, and I asked him to help us out, so he did. He suggested that we make more of that guy. So, we worked him in throughout the movie. Strangely enough, it was Universal that wanted to finally show that guy at the end, but I refused!"

In April of 1966, Andy returned to his boyhood home on Haymore Street in Mount Airy to finalize details of moving his parents to California. Andy told a *Mount Airy News* reporter he was bringing his mother and father to the West Coast so it would be more convenient for him to take care of them.

The home Andy built for the elder Griffiths was only 20 minutes away from his own place—close enough to be neighborly, but far enough away for parents and son to maintain their own lives. Other than missing some life-long friends and relatives, Andy's

Andy and his parents

parents were excited about the move. His mother, Geneva, hoped to now see more of her celebrity son, his wife, and the grandchildren on a regular basis, and Andy thought the new environment might prove beneficial to his father's asthma.

The move was kept simple. Other than personal belongings and some sentimental pieces of furniture Carl had created with his own hands, the bulk of the household was donated to the Salvation Army. The house and the family automobile were sold.

The Griffith family boarded a plane for California and flew cross country to their new home. Except for the rare visit, they would not be coming back.

The transition from the East Coast to the West took some time. Andy's mother had a rougher time getting adjusted. After a few days in California, Carl called his son and told him Geneva was crying. When Andy asked why, his mother told him she couldn't sleep... she wanted her old bed from Mount Airy.

Andy complied. In less than a week, the bed was delivered.

In a North Carolina themed article written for *The Ford Times* published in the April, 1967 issue, Andy was reflective about his early days in his home state:

"To mix up an old saying a bit, you can take a man out of North Carolina, but you can't take North Carolina out of the boy that still lives in the man. I own property there, where the Christmas trees are growing, and I own a lot of memories there which are even more important. Especially as you grow older.

"I was back there (in Mount Airy) a little bit ago and was asked to speak to a little drama group at the high school where I went. Except it's not the same high school I went to. They've built a new one since. Anyway, I was signing my name to things, like you have to in my line of work, when I heard a voice say, 'Mr. Griffith, do you remember Sally Ann Mason?' Only that wasn't the name he said.

"Well, you know how fast the mind can work except when you're being paid for it. In that split second it took before I answered him, my whole life history with Sally Ann Mason went through my head because we went together in school and carved hearts on trees and finally drifted apart the way most heart-carvers do eventually.

"Then I looked up a little from what I was signing and looked up a little more and finally straightened up and right out ahead of me there was this boy tall as I am. 'I'm her son,' he said.

"That's when you know you're getting older."

In a later interview given in 1967, Andy also acknowledged the personal growth he was experiencing:

"Yes, I've changed since I left home. I'm glad I did. I've lived in so many places and crossed paths with so many people. Every now and then a good friend from back home—the best man at our wedding—phones. He'll be a little gassed—and get mad because I don't sound like I used to. But I found out you don't need an accent to tell a story. I realized it when I got a letter from a lady, a teacher, who said she liked the show a lot, but asked if it was necessary to use an accent and incorrect grammar."

As the season ended in mid-1967, Andy commented on his reputation as "a door-puncher" that he was trying no longer to keep things held inside that bothered him regarding the show.

"You know, I'll never have an ulcer. I release my tensions. I holler... stomp... laugh loud. If something bothers me I say so; maybe not right away, but eventually. Fortunately, I'm in a position where I can do it—not everyone is—but I don't do it to hurt anybody."

Part of releasing his tensions included a change of venue. After eight years in Mayberry, Griffith was exhausted. He was ready for something different... and when Universal Studios came calling, Andy was listening. An offer was made that he couldn't refuse. Having already lured away Don Knotts, the executives at Universal were now after the sheriff himself.

"Come with us and make feature films and you'll be another Jimmy Stewart or Hank Fonda," they said, and the powers that be at Universal backed up their words with the lure of a five-year, ten-movie contract.

It had been over six years since Andy had last appeared in a motion picture, and the real star of *The Second Time Around* had been Debbie Reynolds. Longer still since the *Onionhead* fiasco and the easy success of the movie version of *No Time For Sergeants*.

Andy knew his first movie was still his best. *A Face In The Crowd*, while not the biggest financial blockbuster in the history of Warner Brothers, was critically acclaimed during its release and had aged into a modern classic. His performance in the film was enough to silence anyone who thought that Andy Griffith was only capable of doing comedy.

After all, his television work, while enormously popular with the public hadn't been responded to by his peers. Don Knotts took home five Emmys and Francis Bavier one, but Griffith was never even nominated.

"It never bothered me not to win, but I was glad for Don to win," Griffith told an interviewer. "I would have liked for our show to have won. Our show was nominated a couple of times but it never won. I would like the show to have won because I happen to believe that our show at times was very fine."

In 1985, Don Knotts kiddingly added a post script about Griffith's lack of Emmy Awards and how it was never a problem between them, "Andy's not that kind of guy. Besides, he owned the major part of the show, so I got the Emmys, but he got the money!"

So, while Andy was ready to step down from the show that bore his name, the sponsors still wanted to keep Mayberry alive. You can't have Andy's name in the title without Andy, so *Mayberry R.F.D.* was created. CBS even allowed the Andy-less Mayberry to remain in the same Monday night time slot with Ken Berry stepping into the newly-created lead role of Sam Jones, a farmer who had been elected president of Mayberry's Town Council.

"After all, wouldn't you try to salvage something out of one of the most popular shows in television?" commented a CBS executive.

As the *Griffith* show wound down, Sam Jones was introduced in a series of appearances to help ease the transition. The revamped show kept a place in the top ten, Andy and Linke remained the principal owners, and everyone was happy. Now, Andy could focus on returning to his film career.

But what would be his first project? After nearly a decade of being Sheriff Taylor, Griffith believed the public would not be prepared to see him in another Lonesome Rhodes role. So, a decision was made to try and stay close to Andy's roots and not drastically alter his current image (at least not right away).

The project selected was *Angel In My Pocket*—a warm, folksy story about an ex-marine turned country preacher in a small town. While the plot was more "relevant" than a typical episode of *The Andy Griffith Show*, there were still enough similarities to Mayberry to maintain a link.

Angel In My Pocket

The movie's screenplay was by the team of Everett Greenbaum and Jim Fritzell, two of *The Andy Griffith Show's* finest writers. The team had also written the Universal movies, *The Ghost and Mr. Chicken*, *The Reluctant Astronaut*, and *The Shakiest Gun in the West* for Don Knotts. Andy knew both men and trusted their ability to write for his strengths.

Then, the first setback in Griffith's career since the 1950s occurred.

Angel In My Pocket was not well-received and ultimately was not a money maker. In fact, even by 1969 standards the film could be termed as a box-office bomb. A panicky Universal decided that Andy's second picture for them would be a buddy picture called *Me And My Shadow*. Greenbaum and Fritzell were called in to script and as co-star Universal wanted... Don Knotts.

"That cut it," Griffith said when presented with the offer. "I love Don, but teaming up with him again would be like going backwards."

When he asked where the plans to make him into another Jimmy Stewart had gone, Griffith couldn't get a straight answer. Universal had made their decision. Hurt over their lack of confidence, Andy got on the phone with Dick Linke and told his manager to get him out of the deal.

For the first time in 15 years, Andy Griffith was free from any contractual engagements. He saw it as being unemployed. He spent a year doing television guest shots (his last special for CBS was titled ironically enough, *Looking Back*), and live personal appearances, but missed the regularity of an on-going commitment. Finally, he had the downtime to take a lengthy sabbatical in Manteo with Barbara and the children... but spent much of it brooding about the sudden turn his career had taken.

Recalling a speech he made during this slow time to the June, 1970 graduating class at Manteo High School, Andy had this to say:

*Andy and Barbara
fishing near Manteo*

"I talked to them about alternatives... I told them how I always found an alternative for myself when things didn't work. In school, I never was any good at studies or athletics, so I learned to play the horn. In college, I couldn't read music, so I learned to sing a little and I taught glee club later. In New York, when a man told me I couldn't sing, I learned to tell a joke. I kept striving for some way to function, and when I was fortunate enough to have Elia Kazan as my director in *A Face In The Crowd*, I learned how to act."

Andy paused for a moment, and then spoke a thought that had probably raced through his mind throughout the entire deal with Universal. "*A Face In The Crowd*. I wish I could get a role like that again. It'll come along."

Richard Linke was worried for his friend. He knew he had to get Andy back to work as soon as possible, and in a role different from his old "Sheriff Taylor" image. Without Griffith's knowledge,

Linke met with the CBS brass and let them know that their former top-ten star might be interested in returning to television.

"They were so enthralled at the idea of getting Andy again that they offered us one of the most fantastic deals in the history of television," Linke later said. "They signed us for a half-hour weekly series even though we had no script, not even a format in mind. They were willing to take Andy in *anything*. We could have given them a dirty picture if we'd wanted to. And with not one word on paper, we got a contract for five years at $3.5 million a year."

When Linke went to Andy with the deal, there was no hesitation. If the movies weren't ready for the new Andy Griffith, then perhaps television was.

But even Andy was concerned about the image shift.

"You can't be apple pie anymore," Linke told Andy during a meeting soon after the deal with CBS was signed.

"Why can't I be apple pie?" Andy glumly replied.

"Because I want a new image for you: the John Wayne or Henry Fonda type of guy," Linke responded.

With Universal's promises of changing his image ringing in Andy's ears, the actor was concerned, but the challenge of creating a new character and show soon caused Andy's worries to fade.

Teaming with Aaron Ruben, the pair came up with *Headmaster*. Andy liked the concept because he would handle the lead role as a stern but fair school principal, while leaving most of the comedy to Jerry Van Dyke and Parker Fennelly.

"It wasn't easy," Ruben said at the time in discussing a new series vehicle for Andy. "What do you do with a parental sheriff figure with a strongly established image? After awhile, I realized that where it's happening today is on school and college campuses."

"I resisted for several days," Andy admitted. "Because there are two school shows already on TV (*The Bill Cosby Show* and *Room 222*). They're both good, too. But, that's where the action is today—in the schools. That's where the concern is."

Taking stories from the then-current headlines, *Headmaster* aimed at being "hip." With Griffith as the lead, the shows took on the timely concerns of America's troubled youth. Andy was a warm, "fatherly" figure who did his level best to guide his teenage charges through the complex problems of the early 1970s.

"We will do some stories on things like drugs, the generation gap, and other modern themes. But we won't lose sight of comedy. *Headmaster* will be essentially a comedy show. That's what I do best," Andy noted before the show's premiere.

With his strong background in both dramatic and comedic acting, Andy handled the sometimes mawkish storylines well, bringing believability to his scenes. However, the scripts and his supporting cast were not up to his level, and as a whole the series is remembered today as an ambitious failure.

Ratings-wise, the public let it be known they didn't care for *Headmaster*. Ultimately, the series sank to 48th place in the Nielsens. While not a total fiasco, the show was a disappointment considering Griffith's drawing power and the amount of money being spent.

According to an article in *TV Guide*, the show became known in the broadcasting industry as "The $3,500,000 Misunderstanding." Industry insiders believed part of the reason for the show's failure was that Griffith spent a good deal of screen time pompously moralizing with mini-sermons on drug addiction and freedom of academic expression... with little or no time devoted to the "Andy" viewers expected to see.

91

Finally, in a last minute move of desperation coupled with Griffith's own survival instincts (Andy was well aware the show he had envisioned wasn't working out as hoped), the format of *Headmaster* was completely scrapped. CBS wanted to cancel the series? Fine. Andy would serve as his own mid-season replacement.

"The man I was playing was of the academic world," Griffith noted about revamping *Headmaster*. "That is not my world.... I was out of my bag. I couldn't handle it.... I always had a mental block about school. I was always afraid I wouldn't measure up, so I couldn't measure up."

He continued: "There were other things wrong (with the show) too. We were trying to deal with all the big, serious problems, but we didn't have any answers. Before it went on the air, I thought it was going to be a giant hit. By the second show, I had very nervous doubts. By the third, I knew we were in trouble. We knew CBS was unhappy too.... We offered to come up with a whole new show and they told us to go ahead."

One week *Headmaster* would be in the time slot, but the next would feature a show with the title of *The New Andy Griffith Show*, where once again Andy would dispense comedy and wisdom to a small North Carolina town.

His new show was not set up to be innovative—instead, it was nothing more than an updated version of the original *Andy Griffith Show*. Andy was a mayor this time instead of a sheriff, but the basic format was the same... with one major change.

The New Andy Griffith Show included an on-screen wife for Andy in the form of actress and former Miss America Lee Meriwether. A close friend of Griffith's, Meriwether was brought in since she had previously played wife to Andy in *Angel In My Pocket*, and Griffith had been pleased with her talent and their on-screen chemistry .

Meriwether was glad to be involved with the new show, but also aware of Andy's disappointment over the failure of *Headmaster*.

"Andy was faced with an in-between role," she remarked in a 1971 interview. "It wasn't dramatic and it wasn't funny, and Andy just wasn't prepared. He's a marvelous dramatic actor, most people don't realize that, and he's a master of comedy."

At the time, Andy took the blame for *Headmaster's* failure:

"The truth, plain and simple, is that I was lousy. I wasn't comfortable playing a sophisticated educator. I couldn't identify with him. I realize now that every time I played a successful character in the past, that character always had the same roots. First, he was a Southerner. Second, he was based on things I knew in my dumb little town in North Carolina. So that's what I've gone back to. It's the big letter 'C' for comedy, but *regional* comedy—a small point of view which I understand... if people want to call me a rube, I don't care."

So, a man who had earlier refused to make a film with Don Knotts for fear of repeating himself now felt he had to feature his old friend in the very first episode of his new show that kicked off on January 8, 1971. Andy was now "Andy Sawyer," a mayor, husband and father of two living in Greenwood, North Carolina.

For added good measure, George Lindsey and Paul Hartman were also guest stars playing their familiar characters of Goober Pyle and Emmett Clark the Fix-It Man, but oddly enough, no mentions of Mayberry were made. Viewers were led to believe the characters lived some distance away (presumably in Mayberry), but the plot centered around land due to be rezoned in Andy's new setting of Greenwood.

Both Goober and Emmett wanted mayor Andy to help them get the land, but if they lived in Mayberry... why would they need land in Greenwood? A tired looking Griffith looks as confused as the viewer as he struggles with the problem.

Then, to make the premiere episode even more surreal, Don Knotts pulls up at Andy's house wearing his trademark "salt and pepper" suit. Don greets Andy in character... but no mention is made of Barney Fife. "Oh, you," Andy calls him, but a name is never given. Knotts does talk of living in Raleigh and drops other hints... but then, for some unknown reason, also wants the land!

"I really found out that an audience wants you to do what they expect you to do," Andy noted dryly about the revamp, but the public wasn't buying. After all, the word "new" really didn't apply to the show since the same plots and stories had already been done better the first time around... and by the second episode, Goober, Barney and Emmett had departed (without the land).

At the end of the season, after a mere ten episodes, *The New Andy Griffith Show* was canceled.

Another blow came when CBS, in a spate of wanting to rid itself of what was termed to be "rural comedies" (the network was known by the nickname of "The *Hee-Haw* Network") canceled the still enormously popular *Mayberry R.F.D.*—a show that was rated sixth in the Nielsens. Other shows that got the ax included *The Beverly Hillbillies*, *Green Acres*, and, of course, *Hee-Haw*.

"*Headmaster* was a very bad show," Andy said after the cancellation. "And because of *Headmaster*, *The New Andy Griffith Show* simply did not have an audience. But when *Mayberry R.F.D.* was canceled it was as if a very important member of my family had died. I mourned it for years."

Linke shopped *Mayberry R.F.D.* to the other two networks, and even looked into taking the show into first-run syndication with brand new episodes, but was unable to save the show. Ironically, the producers of *Hee-Haw* were able to place their show into syndication, where it thrived and became an even bigger hit.

Andy picked himself up, and began to plot his next move. To keep active, he accepted an engagement at Caesar's Palace in Las Vegas, but even then couldn't find enough new suitable material to perform. After all, a 45-year-old Griffith had little interest in coming out and launching into his bumpkin routines of yore.

That was then, and this was now, and even though attendance wasn't as heavy as it had been in earlier Vegas shows during the height of *The Andy Griffith Show*, Andy was able to content himself with playing the second largest room in town.

"I threw out every bit of the material I bought for the night-club show. I don't know what it is, but I can't find anybody to write for me. My memory of the South is very specific—those (Mount Airy) churches and the way those people are—are very specific in my mind," Andy said of his return to Vegas.

In a revealing 1971 interview, Griffith had this to say:

"I go on interviews for jobs just like everybody else. I'm looking for one, and I don't mind talking about it.... what we're trying to do now is turn me around. It's like starting all over again. I want to become an actor and play character parts. It'll be a long time before I play the lead. I can play heavy anytime... what Dick (Linke) and I will have to do is keep going around seeing people until we find the property that works for us. That's the way we found *No Time For Sergeants* and we'll just have to do the same thing now."

So, Andy began to find jobs as a villain. First came a well-received guest shot as a heavy on *The Mod Squad*. He decided to focus on playing character parts, but the going was slow. The specter of Sheriff Taylor still loomed large in most casting directors' memories.

"I fell out of fashion," Griffith later recalled. "The phone didn't ring much."

Things were also troubled at home—more so than ever before. Despite what had once appeared to be a perfect marriage, Andy and Barbara decided to end their partnership. In 1972, after 23 years of marriage, they were divorced. The papers became final in Santa Monica, California.

"Andy's a millionaire," Richard Linke later commented. "Even though his divorce cost him half of what he had."

As for other details of the settlement, Andy kept his own council and Barbara did likewise.

❧◉☙

After his *Mod Squad* appearance, Andy began to move into TV movies. First was *The Strangers In 7-A*, a melodrama where he portrayed a meek apartment house manager:

"I played a loser... with Ida Lupino in (*7-A*) and there was this scene where this young girl took his shirt off and started dancing around him. It was a very seductive scene. And when the show came on the air, my father said, 'You oughtn't had been in the room with that girl.' I said, 'Daddy, I was just acting,' and he said, 'I don't care what you was doing, you oughtn't a been in the room with her.' "

This was followed by *Go Ask Alice*, which was a critically-acclaimed adaptation of the famous, yet downbeat young adult novel about a young teenager trying to find her way back after an overdose of LSD. Then came a third project, where Andy was mentioned for the role of Sam Farragut, a character the actor called "a severely evil, driven man." If playing "heavies" would help him escape typecasting, Andy was more than willing to take on the work:

"A part came up in a picture for television called *Pray For The Wildcats*. There was one scene in particular that made me decide to

96

take the part—it was an almost rape scene in a Mexican cantina. It was a young girl, and when my name came up about that part, the producer said, 'He can't play that.' The casting director said, 'Didn't you ever see *A Face In The Crowd?*"

The casting director won out and Andy was chilling in the film. However, his Mayberry ties were still there. On the night before shooting a scene where the Farragut character gets drunk and lusts after a young girl, Griffith suffered a terrifying nightmare that he had literally beaten Don Knotts to death with his bare hands.

"It was vivid," Andy later remarked, an involuntary shiver running through his body as he remembered the dream. "His head was just swinging there. I had people get rid of the body. Then, I woke up, wet all over. I immediately called Don, but he couldn't be found.... I'm sure part of the dream was an expression of my self-doubt at that time. But the biggest message was quite simple: I was trying to kill the image of Sheriff Taylor and everything connected with it. I had to kill it, you see, or I wasn't going to get work—which would have *truly* killed me."

Griffith called his psychologist ("I'm not ashamed of the fact that I go to a shrink when things get tough") and his theory behind the dream was confirmed.

"It was difficult at first to break that (mold) because of the nature of our town out there," Andy continued, referring to Hollywood. "If you do one thing and it is successful, they tend to figure that's it for you. I got lucky and got a few roles that were just so far the other way. Now, I have to be careful on that score.... In my trade you have to constantly take several steps back before you can take one forward. You have to be able to cope with failure constantly. I've done many things that I thought should work."

Audience reaction ranged from shock to outright disbelief. Many letters from Mayberry fans were received in Richard Linke's office wanting to know what Andy was thinking by playing such a role.

"... I just had to do that one—it just had to be done," Andy said in 1974. "One reviewer praised the movie and said that 'Andy Griffith is a good actor.' I want to be considered just that by audiences. I loved the old *Andy* series, but I cannot sit around and think back to them and do nothing else. I want to stay busy, not sit on the sidelines and remember how good it used to be. I can't mourn the loss of the old shows."

1973 also saw the syndicated broadcast premiere of *This Is Your Life: Andy Griffith*. Richard Linke worked with *This Is Your Life* host Ralph Edwards to assemble the tribute. Linke then lead an unsuspecting Andy into the ambush. When the surprise was sprung, Griffith was reportedly furious. He felt totally unprepared. The methodical actor hated being placed in a situation without any rehearsal or material.

However, once he calmed down and saw Linke meant well, Andy tried to relax and enjoy the mix of family members like his mother and father, old friends such as Garnett Steele and Ed Mickey from Mount Airy, and current celebrity pal Ken Berry. Ron Howard was also on hand to talk about the lessons learned by playing Opie Taylor opposite his "Pa," while Jim Nabors spoke about how the chance to play Gomer Pyle was his big break.

In addition to filming *Wildcats* in 1973, Andy showed up in the usual array of specials and variety shows, including a musical-comedy review titled *NBC Follies* where he shared the stage with Sammy Davis, Jr., John Davidson, Mickey Rooney and Connie Stevens and an inspired bit where he played a singing used car salesman on *The Flip Wilson Show*.

1974 got off to a chilly start for Andy as he spent 25 days on top of Southern California's 7800-foot-high Big Bear Mountain filming *Winter Kill*, an ABC TV-movie and pilot. Thanks to the 60-

degree incline of the mountain's face, the only transportation up and down consisted of snowmobiles. The crew was forced to improvise a number of ways to keep their equipment and themselves from freezing in the multiple snowstorms experienced during the three-week shoot. Cameras—and their operators—were kept under heavy quilts.

While the frigid weather added to the realism of the fictional ski-resort setting of Andy's role as Sheriff Sam Adams, the actor himself was heard to comment between chattering teeth, "If it becomes a series, can we shoot in Malibu?"

However, after he was able to climb back down the mountain, Andy looked upon *Winter Kill* as an enjoyable—if somewhat trying—experience:

"I was pleased with the character (of Adams). I had never played anything like it before. We had a lot of script trouble in the film, though, and I got a little discouraged from time to time.... But a couple of days ago I saw the finished product, and I must say that when I saw how well it held together I was very pleased."

When asked if he preferred television to movies, Andy responded, "Well, if there were still a lot of movies to be made, and if a man could spend three or four months making one, then I would say I prefer movies. But that situation is not realistic these days. All of that is in the past. So, inasmuch as I like to work on a regular basis, I would say television is the place for me."

Andy was uncertain as to how ABC would approach a potential series. Malibu locations or not, Andy was willing to commit depending on what the network wanted. ABC did spend a great deal of time and money promoting the film and was rewarded with high ratings. However, only two episodes of the series, *Adams Of Eagle Lake* were produced and shown, and much to Griffith's disappointment the idea of pursuing the character on a weekly basis was abandoned.

But during what now seemed to be an endless string of television movies, Andy was cast to perfection as the cynical Howard Pike in the 1975 motion picture *Hearts Of The West*. The film centered around Lewis Tater, a young man from Iowa who ends up falling in with a small film company specializing in cranking out cheap B-westerns.

Andy played the weary stunt coordinator for the fictional movie company, serving as Tater's less-than-honest mentor. Critics were quick to point to Griffith's work as being top-notch, but except for a warm reception on the midnight movie and college circuit, the film never found an audience. Today, this little movie is considered to be a cult classic.

Another reason given for why *Hearts Of The West* failed to find an audience during the initial release was partly because of charges that a movie mogul character played by Donald Pleasence was anti-Semitic. The controversy hurt the movie, newspapers wouldn't allow the film to be advertised, and ultimately *Hearts* was never able to recover from what proved to be unfair accusations.

"*Hearts Of The West* got good reviews all over the country; all over the world it got good reviews. And you could have shot a cannon off anywhere it played—while *Mahogany* was a real piece of s—t, and they were standing around the block to get in. What do you do? Go to bat again next chance you get," Andy once commented angrily about how the film was buried.

In addition to being disappointed over his performance being overlooked, Andy took a financial loss on the film. He netted only a few hundred dollars for his work since he signed a contract for a percentage of the profits.

Hearts Of The West

Also in 1975, the city of Mount Airy leased the old Rockford Street School to the Surry Arts Council. The school had been used in later years as a gymnasium and auditorium for the town, but the new owners had other ideas, including remodeling the structure into a small, yet fully functional theatre and arts center.

The Surry Arts Council acquired a $330,000 federal public works grant to pay for the project. The refurbished building featured an auditorium that could seat 350 people and the stage (which once was used for basketball games) received an orchestra pit. A new lighting and sound system was added, while the main school building was torn down to provide room for parking.

On the very same boards that Andy had once trod in high school and opera club productions, a new generation of actors and performers would now be given the opportunity to shine in the newly christened "Andy Griffith Playhouse."

Always embarrassed at this sort of attention, Andy agreed to lend his name to the new building, and released a brief statement of gratitude that was later reprinted in the program for the Mount Airy Community Theatre's 1976 production of *Fiddler On The Roof*.

"There is a need in all of us for self-expression, and I am glad that the artistic talents of the young people in Mount Airy are being recognized and developed through the efforts of the Surry Arts Council. The opportunities for learning and performing at the old Rockford Street School merit the full support of the community.

"I am pleased and honored that the people of Mount Airy have named its community theatre after me. This gesture of affection is deeply appreciated."

Andy also gave financial support as well to the fledgling Surry Arts Council, but as always kept the amount, and any subsequent publicity this act might have generated, to himself.

Tragedy also struck in 1975, when Andy's father died at the age of 79. "My father," Andy remembered, "My father was a brilliant man.... He was brilliant and he had a wonderful sense of humor and he was so good, he was such a good strong man. Wonderful model. The only thing he did wrong was he smoked every breath. And it killed him."

Early 1976 saw Andy popping up with every celebrity who had a variety show. First, in March, was a spot on *Tony Orlando And Dawn* where Andy played a farmer and sang a tune about his experiences with UFOs and aliens.

Then, in April, Andy showed up as the featured guest on the hour-long weekly comedy *The Rich Little Show*. Andy joined Rich in comedy sketches involving soap operas, tax consultants, psychiatrists, bathtub commanders and Inspector Clumseau.

August brought Griffith to Frankie Avalon's four-week short lived summer series, *Easy Does It*. Avalon wisely used Griffith in several comedy blackout bits and let him sing a medley of country songs.

Andy even replaced Burl Ives as narrator for the second Frosty the Snowman Christmas special, *Frosty's Winter Wonderland*. A Disneyland children's record of music and dialogue from the show was also released.

But the stand-out project during this year was a role in the ABC mini-series *Washington: Behind Closed Doors*. Andy knew he had a terrific part in Esker Anderson, and he took the character and ran with it. In one scene with Cliff Robertson, Andy had to remember a ten-page monologue while confronting his fellow actor:

"(It took) an arm and a leg's worth of energy. I had first to learn the scene, then I had to draw the meaning of the character and what he was driving at in those moments. And then, I had to build up the necessary energy to play with," Andy said of the performance that even caused the set crew to break out in applause. "Every now and then, something wonderful happens on-stage. You don't ever fear, you're right on the mark. All the time. You can tell that, and so can everybody else."

After the long, intense speech, the set crew began to applaud, and when the series aired, so did the critics. By this time, Griffith was content with such showcase roles: "It's not a necessity for me that I play a lead role—thank God I don't have that kind of ego. But it is a necessity that the part be interesting."

However, always searching for another series vehicle, Andy did co-produce (with MGM and Richard Linke) two television movies in 1977 featuring the character of Abel Marsh. The first was *The Girl In The Empty Grave* and the second *Deadly Game* (which had been filmed under the working title *It's Deadly*). Both were whimsical murder mysteries set in a resort town in the California mountains, but unlike the earlier, and much grimmer, *Winter Kill*, the setting of Jasper Lake was warm and sunny.

"There's this small town," Andy explained to an interviewer. "Something horrendous happens, and all these ordinary people try to figure it out. And at the same time, they talk about having to borrow the car to go to the doctor, about dress sales, and whether they slept well, and whether the coffee was good. Because it is a small town, they go about things the way people do in a small town."

Both movies were popular, with *The Girl In The Empty Grave* winning in its time slot. However, like ABC and *Winter Kill*, NBC passed on making *Abel Marsh* a regular series.

In the Fall of 1978, Andy was asked to be the featured speaker at the University of North Carolina at Chapel Hill's Annual University Day, which took place on October 12. The ceremony commemorates the laying of the cornerstone of the Old East building in 1793, and features the presentation of Distinguished Alumnus Awards.

Andy had been back on campus in 1977 when driving alone from Manteo to Mount Airy. He had stopped in Chapel Hill for the night and felt the pangs of nostalgia for his college days. Donning a cap as a disguise, Andy wandered the grounds under the cover of darkness—finding himself near the buildings and area where he had spent so much of his time. There he saw the Playmakers Theatre and Memorial Hall, which unleashed a torrent of memories.

Griffith approached a guard and with the help of some savvy students who had recognized him, talked security into unlocking the doors and letting him enter Memorial where he wanted to see the grand old chandelier. The stage in Memorial marked his first Chapel Hill appearance on stage in *The Gondoliers*, and for a brief moment, Andy saw himself as a young man once more.

Now, a year later, Andy Griffith's time had arrived to be recognized by his former alma mater. After a humorous morning address, Andy was surprised when Ferebee Taylor, the university chancellor, presented him with the award.

"Andy Griffith may be the most widely known and recognized alumnus of this institution," said Taylor. "He certainly is the only person ever who, almost single-handedly, added a whole new town to the Tar Heel state—Mayberry, as everybody knows, that friendly little place near Mount Airy where Griffith was born.... Andy Griffith has never quite lost the tar off of his heels. Moreover, for millions of people all over America, he remains, as Sheriff Andy Taylor, the typical North Carolinian."

*Andy speaks at
UNC-Chapel Hill*

"It's wonderful to be working with something you love, and these people got me there," Griffith said afterward about his college drama and music teachers. "... I did graduate from here. It took me five years and two summers, though. That's nothing to be proud of—I just didn't know."

He paid homage to Paul Young, director of the Glee Club where Andy's bass-baritone always took the line "Five Golden Rings" in "The Twelve Days of Christmas," and to Foster Fitz-Simons of the Department of Dramatic Arts where Andy honed his dramatic skills, and to Preston Epps, who taught Andy Greek and led him in the University Methodist Choir.

"There was some special quality about (Andy)," remembered his classmate Jane Rogers, Class of 1948, who was also in the campus Glee Club. "I didn't know him personally, really, yet he is the only person from Glee Club who stands out in my mind."

On Monday, February 5, 1979, Andy was able to return to his spoken word recording roots as one of the hosts of the *Sears Radio Theatre* on the CBS Radio Drama Network. CBS presented radio plays each weeknight, Monday through Friday. Andy was joined in his hosting duties by Richard Widmark, Cicely Tyson and Vincent Price. There was a different theme each night: Westerns on Monday; Comedy on Tuesday; Mystery on Wednesday; Love & Hate on Thursday; Adventure on Friday. Unfortunately, this innovative series was largely overlooked.

1979 also brought another prime-time series to Griffith in the form of a science-fiction/adventure series *Salvage-1*. "I thought it was Saturday morning television," Andy said. "Until I looked closer at the creativity and possibilities involved."

Quick to dismiss earlier ventures such as *Headmaster* or *The New Andy Griffith Show*, Andy has always spoken fondly of *Salvage-1*:

"I particularly like the fact the show is action and adventure, but without any violence and with a lot of humor. And my character, Harry Broderick, is a successful proprietor of a scrap yard who does not believe in the word impossible.... Harry is a man with a dream. He is the catalyst who makes the wildest schemes possible—whether it's salvaging Apollo hardware from the surface of the moon or searching the globe for near-extinct dwarf spider monkeys priced at $30,000 each.

"It's not going to change the face of television, but we do have a chance to do something different. It's delightful nonsense—and it's nonviolent."

When given the script for the first two-hour *Salvage-1* movie, Andy had no intention of doing a series. "I read it and I liked it very much. I thought it was just for a TV movie, but they said they might do a series. I said, 'No, I'll just do the movie.' We had an impasse. Then, finally, I said to myself, 'Well, it probably won't sell anyway, so I'll do it. And I did it and here we are and I'm glad."

Salvage-1 proved to be a sometimes charming, sometimes silly science fiction program that showcased Andy's talents. After all, it's not everyday Andy Griffith gets to go up against a Bigfoot or search for a lost World War II bomber and find a Japanese pilot who isn't aware the war is long over.

Andy kept his usual routines while filming the series, getting up at 5:30 to study his script, dress and drive himself to the studio. "I guess I'm a bit like Harry, the character I play in *Salvage-1*... a dreamer, loyal to friends but also a con artist who will take advantage of a situation," he said. "He likes humor when it's appropriate, but he has a very serious side."

In his first series since *The New Andy Griffith Show*, Andy found his temper had cooled, but was by no means dormant. A Griffith explosion could still be triggered by the right catalyst. "He doesn't do it as much as he used to," said Richard Linke at the time. "Andy has matured in that way. But if he decides to let it out, everybody better watch out!"

In a *People Weekly* profile written during filming of *Salvage-1*, a list was given of things that drove Andy crazy. As on *The Andy Griffith Show*, the always professional Griffith could not and would not tolerate late actors who kept scenes waiting, actors who did not know their lines, and actors who tried to perform under the influence of alcohol.

Andy has also never been enthralled with directors who didn't listen to his suggestions and tell him exactly what they wanted in a scene. If they tried to brush him aside with promises or platitudes, Andy noted that "I really lose my cool. I don't trust anybody on my work. I want to know what I'm doing all the time—and why."

Salvage-1 was never given a real chance to find an audience, being shown in different time slots on different days. The show was even taken off the air for months and then brought back as a mid-season replacement before being canceled.

The year also featured another cancellation for Andy. In 1975, he had married Greek actress Solicia Cassuto, but divorced her in 1979. "A union definitely not made in heaven," Andy later said of his second marriage. "I continued after I married her to live by myself."

The newly single Griffith was on the roof of his home in North Hollywood repairing a leak in early 1980, when the earth moved. Andy noticed his tools start to slide down past him. "Then," he

109

stated about the mishap, "*I* started to slide off. I made one lunge for a big tree limb, missed and hit the ground in a sitting position about 20 feet later. I remember an extraordinary shot of pain going through my body, then I passed out."

Andy's back was broken. Orthopedic specialists were able to repair the damage to his lumbar vertebrae without limiting Griffith's movements too much... although they told him to stay off the roof, and avoid any heavy lifting. The accident ended up taking a quarter-inch off Andy's height. With such a debilitating injury, the first half of 1980 found Griffith recovering from the injury in Manteo.

The rest of the year was spent filming *Murder In Texas*, a dramatization of the murder case of Doctor John Hill, a Houston plastic surgeon accused of killing his first wife by the woman he marries afterward. Andy played Ash Robinson, the father whose daughter was murdered. Convinced of his former son-in-law's guilt, the wealthy Robinson spends every waking moment attempting to find the evidence needed to convict Doctor Hill.

For his work, Andy was finally nominated for an Emmy Award in 1981—his first and only nomination. He did not return from the awards presentation a winner. Afterward, he commented:

"I was disappointed in not winning the Emmy not so much for anything else except you feel like such a damn fool sitting there on TV. I didn't stand a chance anyway. I've never won anything in my life and never expect to. I'm not angry about that. Some people do and some don't.... I'm told I've been overlooked, but at the same time I get a few... juicy parts every year or two so... I don't know, I've had a pretty good run at it.... It would be nice to have one when my mother comes over or a cousin comes to visit, but I can manage without it."

1982 was a quiet, uneventful year spent working on a forgotten pilot called *For Lovers Only* and a new movie for television, *Murder*

In Coweta County. However, 1983 presented Andy with an emotional roller coaster ride that forever altered his life and his perception of living.

The year had begun promisingly with Andy wedding Cindi Knight, whom he met in 1978 in Manteo during the annual production of *The Lost Colony.* Andy was in the audience, but spotted the actress and later introduced himself. A native from Jacksonville, Florida, the vivacious Cindi was also a dancer and former teacher... a background Andy knew well, and it gave them common ground:

"I met her and we subsequently became friends. And I knew her as a friend a long time before, as people will, we started dating and then seeing one another on a day-to-day basis.... I know a lot of guys say this, but she is the best thing that ever happened to me.... This woman has brought me more joy than I've ever known. Not jiggling, dancing around joy. I mean deep-down-to-my shoes joy."

Most recently, the pair had worked together on the *Coweta County* project, in which Cindi had a small acting part as a mother and witness. The film was shot on location in Griffin, Georgia and created quite a stir when it was discovered that Andy was playing the bad guy murderer John Wallace, not good guy sheriff Lamar Potts.

"Everybody, including Lamar Potts, Jr. (the real life son of the late sheriff in the original case) said they were surprised I wasn't playing the sheriff," Andy said with a laugh on the first day of shooting. "You can see why."

Later, after filming was completed, Andy told Bill King of the *Atlanta Constitution* that the moonshiner was "A marvelous part.... Wallace was carrying a set of emotions that I don't carry and I can't identify with them. So I was doing a pure acting job there."

With time off before starting work on the CBS mini-series *Chiefs,* Andy and Cindi were wed on April 2, 1983 in a private ceremony at the Griffith home in Manteo. This was Andy's third marriage and Cindi's first.

However, six weeks after the marriage, on a Saturday morning in May, Andy woke up next to his new bride in their home in Toluca Lake and realized he was having trouble moving. He'd been suffering the body pains of a viral-like flu for several days, but those minor aches were nothing like this.

He managed to roll over on his side and felt a tingling sensation in his legs and feet. When he tried to raise himself up and get out of bed, he collapsed on the floor. At first Andy thought he might have slept in a strange position and the blood to his lower extremities was cut off. The tingling felt like his legs were "asleep."

When Cindi rushed to her husband's side to help, Andy couldn't stand. He could barely move.

"My muscles wouldn't operate—I couldn't use them to raise up my foot... I was paralyzed, and my wife and I didn't know what was wrong with me," Andy told writer Jerry Buck in an article for *Redbook* magazine in 1989.

Then a searing pain shot through Griffith's unmoving lower limbs and didn't go away. Griffith described it as being "like a hot branding iron." He tried to contact his doctor, but since it was a weekend the physician couldn't be reached. When Cindi proposed going to the emergency room, Andy said no. He decided the pain would go away in a few hours.

Instead, over the next two days, it got worse, and even a man with a dislike of doctors was relieved to finally reach his physician on Monday morning. The response was predictable—the actor was told to check himself into St. Joseph Medical Center in Burbank immediately.

Andy was admitted to the coronary care unit under the fake name of "Samuel Knight." By this time, the tingling had completely vanished and had been replaced with continual pain.

"Cindi and I were met by an army of doctors," Griffith recalled. "I went through all kinds of tests, but I don't remember most of them because I was in so much pain. But I do remember that none of the doctors knew what was wrong with me."

Then, on the fourth day of being hospitalized, two specialists, Gerald Kessler and Richard Anderson, examined the ailing actor and diagnosed him as suffering from Guillain-Barre syndrome, a rare neurological disease that attacks the peripheral nerves and can result in paralysis of the legs, face, arms and even the respiratory system, leaving a victim unable to breathe.

The cause of Guillain-Barre Syndrome is unknown and the length and severity of the illness can not be predicted. Basically, it affects each victim in different ways. Since there is no known cure or treatment, a patient's recovery is always uncertain.

After enduring a spinal tap, evidence of the syndrome was confirmed when it revealed that Andy's blood-protein count was low—a positive indicator of the ailment. Andy was examined for ten days in the hospital—long enough for doctors to determine that while they could do little to help him, at least the condition was not going to get any worse. The disease was not affecting any vital functions, and had stopped at his lower back.

They explained that while the paralysis was usually temporary and the disease would reverse itself, extra attention would have to be given during this critical juncture. The real struggle would come afterward, when Andy would have to face the chore of rebuilding his strength and repairing the damaged muscles.

Andy was sent home, where he spent the next few weeks in a wheelchair taking medication to temporarily ward off the pain. A specialist had told him it might take three years or more before a complete recovery was possible. Visions of spending the rest of his life paralyzed went through his mind.

Andy believed the end of his career had finally come, and he responded by selling off expensive possessions, including his shot-gun collection and one of his classic cars. When Cindi found out she immediately made her husband stop. However, Andy's despair only grew when word came that his lead role in *Chiefs* had been recast with Charlton Heston. Those closest to him feared the actor had given up.

"Andy's first reaction was panic," Richard Linke recalled. "Then when it was diagnosed, he just set about doing what the doctors told him to do."

"I was too sick to work, and I thought I'd never work again. I had atrophied legs, looking about as old as my dad's when he died.... Cindi really took care of me. I truly don't think I could have done it without her," Griffith said in 1990 after his recovery.

Private, as always, Andy told few people outside of his immedi-ate family of his sudden, shocking illness. He would deal with this in his own way, without going public.

His new wife's first act was to convince her husband to fight back. She knew that someone equipped with Andy's own natural tenacity and will power could beat this disease. Matching her deter-mination with his own, Griffith entered the California Northridge Hospital Medical Center in June, 1983 and with Cindi at his side began the journey back.

"Cindi... protected whatever strength and health I had," Griffith said. "She was so kind, driving me to the hospital or wherever I had to go. She'd throw the wheelchair in and out of the car. I would want to help her, but she'd look at me and say, 'Now, Andy, it's easier if you just let me do it.' Cindi helped me to use my strength where it needed to be used."

Andy and Cindi

He stayed at Northridge for nearly two months, learning how to deal with the pain. He attended regular sessions with a psychologist to find out how to cope with his body's new limitations and avoid bouts of depression... and he spent six hours a day in physical therapy learning how to walk again. Andy would sit or lie down as the therapist moved his legs and feet, moving the unfeeling flesh... and for weeks all Andy could do was watch.

Then, one day, in the middle of his daily therapy, Griffith experienced an almost forgotten sensation. He was able to make one of his toes work, moving the tiny digit with a Herculean effort. This was more than a positive sign—this was a full blown miracle. Andy was on his way to regaining muscle control.

"Magnificent people there (at Northridge), as fine as I've ever encountered. They made such a big deal out of moving that toe that I felt kinda proud myself. It beat any standing ovation I ever got," he later told *TV Guide*.

Seven months passed before Andy was able to return home from Northridge, but he returned able to walk again... with the help of two white plastic leg braces that extended down into his shoes. He later said he didn't wear the braces for walking—he wore them to help the pain:

"Once something like this happens, you realize how frail the body is and how resilient the mind is—also how much your spiritual life means to you and how much your friends mean to you."

As he recovered from the disease, Andy decided to make himself more visible. He signed again with the William Morris Agency and would show up unannounced in their offices. He would wait in the lobby, his familiar face and booming voice unmistakable to producers and casting agents as they would come by in search of talent. Perhaps Griffith remembered how the same ploy had won him the role of Will Stockdale almost 35 years earlier by simply hanging around and being himself.

His face-to-face tactics worked. His first job was as spokesperson in print and television for the American Telephone and Telegraph Company (AT&T). Although excited, Andy was so afraid the advertising executives might see the leg braces and believe him to be ill that after meeting them for a working lunch he was scared to get up from the table again:

"I stayed seated because I was afraid my pants had risen and if I stood up, I'd reveal my braces. When the lunch was over and they all got up to leave, I told them I wanted to stay behind and have another cup of coffee."

Oddly enough, the first AT&T television commercial featured

Andy dressed in a checkered shirt and seated in an easy chair as he reassured consumers who were nervous at the time over the battles being fought after the government abolished AT&T's monopoly and opened the playing field. "You know what I'm going to do during the biggest revolution in telephone history? Relax." Andy said.

However, he knew rumors about his paralysis had raced through the entertainment industry, so for the second commercial he told AT&T "It's important to me that you have me walk. So they did."

The commercials were followed by an appearance on the ABC prime time series *Hotel*. Andy took the guest-shot as a test for himself because his character was supposed to be seen jogging. Baggy sweat pants covered his lower legs and feet and Andy did what the role required... even though he was in great pain and had to rest often between takes. However the end result was flawless. When the show aired, there was no evidence anything was wrong with Andy Griffith.

Buying himself a special pair of zip-up boots to cover the braces on his size-14 feet, Griffith began to walk tall, and more offers began to come his way... and except for one special case, they were nothing at all like Andy of Mayberry.

One such offer took Griffith to Almeria, Spain late in 1984 where he co-starred in the western film *Rustler's Rhapsody*. However, this was no ordinary western. This film was a tongue in cheek homage to Gene Autry and Roy Rogers singing cowboy movies.

"I'm playing a cattle baron, and, well, he's gay," Griffith said in a telephone interview from Almeria. "This may be something new for a western: a lead heavy who is gay."

Also in late 1984, Andy had to deal with a campaign launched by 14-year-old Andy Griffith Show Appreciation Society president John Meroney to convince a willing North Carolina small town to change its name to "Mayberry." Meroney alerted the media and began writing letters with every intention of having a real Mayberry in time for the twenty-fifth anniversary of the show...

Until Andy let it be known he was less than excited by the "tribute."

"I just wanted you to know that I had nothing to do with this," Griffith told the *Winston-Salem Journal*. "This all came out of his (Meroney's) head. This whole idea of searching for a town to change its name to Mayberry is enormously embarrassing to me. I have asked him not to pursue it any further."

But 1984 is best remembered for Andy's small, but pivotal role as North Carolina lawyer and prosecutor for the United States Department of Justice Victor Worheide, in the NBC mini-series *Fatal Vision*. In the opening scene where a cranky Griffith is behind his cluttered desk cutting his toenails, viewers knew they were in for something different.

So did NBC Entertainment President Brandon Tartikoff, who decided he liked Griffith as a lawyer and believed there were possibilities for a regular series. Tartikoff sent producers Fred Silverman and Dean Hargrove to see if Andy was interested.

"I'd have to say he had some hesitation," admitted Hargrove later. "Although he liked the idea of the show and he liked the character very much." Ultimately, Andy was willing to attempt another series, and the process of creating *Matlock* was begun.

Asked what the show was going to be about, Andy replied:

"This has to do with a lawyer in Atlanta, and his firm, and his daughter who works with him and the cases they're involved in. Now that doesn't sound like much, but neither does a bigot who lives up north with his wife, and neither does a girl who works for a television station in Minneapolis, and neither does a sheriff in a

118

small town with a skinny deputy. None of the ideas mean anything until they're populated, the script is written and it's really put together. Then you say, 'Oh, I see,' or 'Let's forget it,' one or the other."

Meanwhile, Hargrove, who was writing the pilot, designed Ben Matlock in what he called "the mold of people like Percy Foreman and 'Race Horse' Haynes, the very colorful, shrewd Murder One attorneys who seem to be country boys but who are really sly foxes."

While *Matlock* was in the early stages, Andy also appeared in other roles that allowed him to show off his range. From the summer of 1985 onward, he was a whirlwind of activity.

First off was the chain-smoking, psychotic juvenile court judge in the TV movie *Crimes Of Innocence*. Although on screen for less than twenty minutes, Griffith's work was electrifying as he allowed the corruptness of the judge to slowly shine through in a riveting final sequence where his only prop was a cigarette.

Then, in October of 1985, the *Matlock* pilot film *Diary Of A Perfect Murder* was shot and Andy took to Ben Matlock instantly:

"I have had the best time making this show of any show I've done in a long time... when you can add humor... as I'm able to do with this part, then it gives me everything. I like this character more than any character I have been associated with in years, more than any character since Andy Taylor."

"I didn't work for almost two years," Andy told an Atlanta reporter during the location shooting of *Diary Of A Perfect Murder* in October, 1985. "And it was rough. You begin to feel like you are not needed.... But I'm happy to say I am recovered. I still deal with pain in my feet. And I may always, I don't know. But it's not so I can't stand it."

From *Diary*, Griffith immediately went right into filming another television movie for NBC where he played an alcoholic. *Under The Influence* was a harrowing look at the disease and how it destroys a once loving family.

"I dread it," Andy said when starting the film. "I want to do it, but it's going to be difficult.... Most of the drunks that we see on the screen are comedic drunks. And you get away with a lot of mistakes with that. The reality of it is it's not funny at all. Not a bit."

Finally, in February, 1986, *Return To Mayberry* was put before the cameras and aired by NBC on April 13, 1986. The long-awaited reunion movie was in pre-production for over a year, but it only took a 19-day location shoot in the little town of Los Olivos, California (the original backlot at Culver City long since bulldozed) to bring Mayberry back to life.

The idea for the reunion film was triggered when Andy, Don Knotts and Ron Howard made a joint appearance to present an Emmy Award in 1983. Pleased by the audience response and delight in seeing the three together again, Andy took his former son and deputy out to dinner and discussed getting back together. Howard and Knotts agreed. Griffith then checked with the other residents of Mayberry and found no holdouts among the large cast.

"I think everybody would have been disappointed not to be asked," said Ron Howard.

"I had been approached for a number of years (about a reunion) and I always passed on it," Andy remarked in 1985. "But there has been so much interest of late in the show and about the characters, I thought that while we're all alive we ought to give it one more shot. I want to tell you one thing—it's got to be good—no, it's got to be excellent. Because we did what we did as well as we could do it. It can't be anything that's like, 'Well, let's do it and get it over with.' I won't do it that way."

"The people who run the networks are more or less idiots," Writer Everett Greenbaum said in *America On The Rerun* after *Return* aired to both high ratings and critical acclaim. "Before they came to me, they had spent a lot of money on scripts that were just awful—they were written about people you'd never seen before— the descendants of the original cast. And they were all going to analysts so Andy finally called me and said he was going to run away and hide... (so) I got ahold of Dick Linke, Andy's manager, and I said 'We want everyone in this, anybody who played an interesting or memorable character.'

"Dick Linke said the American public doesn't want to see any-one who's fat and has gray hair, and I said, 'You idiot, that's exactly what they want to see. They want to see how their old friends look now."

Andy and Richard Linke during the original **Andy Griffith Show**

Andy's fears over what *Return* could become were eased by the addition of Greenbaum and Harvey Bullock, who co-wrote the screenplay. Original director Bob Sweeney also was coaxed out of retirement for the film. Other than Francis Bavier, who was ill during the time of shooting, the rest of the surviving original cast was more than happy to come home to Mayberry.

Although everyone admitted it took some time to fall back into the old patterns, Don Knotts commented on how he had to rein himself in as Barney Fife since "... my tendency was to overact a bit at first, because I'd been doing *Three's Company* and they wanted me to do that. So, I had to pull it down a little. Still, there was some apprehension on my part—can I still do that guy? But very quickly it began to feel like old times."

"I had forgotten how to do Gomer," stated Jim Nabors. "We hadn't rehearsed, the cameras were there and I thought, Lord, I don't remember how to do this. It took me about two minutes to get into it. Then it was great fun!"

During the filming of the reunion movie, Griffith recalled "At that time we had so much press and so many cameras around our stage we finally had to make it a closed set. We couldn't work. At one point we had a scene, we had six mini-cams in the set with us."

"They were planning *Matlock* when we were writing *Return To Mayberry*, and *Matlock* would not have gone on if *Return* had not brought in such tremendous numbers," noted Greenbaum.

Greenbaum was correct about the "numbers." *Return To Mayberry* pulled a 34.6 Nielsen rating and a whopping 53 share. More than 28.3 million households, equaling roughly 55 million people, were sitting before their televisions on that Sunday night and watching their old Mayberry friends.

The *Matlock* movie pilot, which had been shown a month earlier, also garnered high ratings—high enough for NBC to green light a series. The new show premiered on September 20, 1986 as an ongoing hour-long courtroom drama. Guest star Dick Van Dyke served as both the killer... and the presiding judge at the trial where the deceased's fiancee has been brought up on murder charges. Ben Matlock to the rescue.

The series was a hit. A top 15 show. With the success of *Matlock*, a second proposed Mayberry movie *Christmas In Mayberry*, never appeared. America had now embraced Andy as a southern Perry Mason... and he was enjoying every moment of the experience.

"I understand that Raymond Burr was passionate about the law in *Perry Mason*," Andy said when discussing the two shows. "I'm not disregarding the law, but my first goal is to entertain. I allow my character of Matlock to do things that I think most lawyers would have been thrown out of court for a long time ago. But I think it's funny and entertaining."

Soon after the show's premiere, a favorable review ran in *TV Guide*, noting that "You have to enjoy Griffith, with his hands in the pockets of his light suit, sauntering around the courtroom with a look of sheer innocence on his face as he sets a trap for a lying witness. There's nothing like a pro to make a show work, and Andy, by golly, is a pro."

However, even a pro needs a break, and unlike most stars who crave every moment before the cameras, Andy asked for more characters to be written into *Matlock* during the 1986-1987 season. Much like Don's Knotts' request for at least four episodes off each season of his tenure on *The Andy Griffith Show*, Griffith needed down time. He logically pointed out that in some episodes he's on screen in virtually every scene.

"It's a difficult job," noted Dean Hargrove. "Andy ultimately has to be the one who handles what happens in the courtroom. That's 20 percent of the show that's entirely his, on top of everything else he does."

Griffith still suffered residual pain from Guillain-Barre Syndrome, especially if he had to stand for long periods of time. He treated himself with aspirin, knowing the temporary discomfort was nothing compared to the agony he suffered when first contracting the disease:

"When I started filming *Matlock* I wasn't sure I could go without my braces. I was afraid I couldn't. Then one day, I decided to try. To tell the truth, it took some courage. I took them off and made it through the day. Then I did it again, and in a few months time, I kept them off for good."

"My feet feel very strange," he commented about other lingering effects of the illness. "It's hard to explain—it's as if they're asleep. I feel it especially when the weather changes. But it's not a crippling pain. I suspect I'll have that feeling for the rest of my life—it's been there so long now that I don't remember what my feet felt like before.

"I owe God a lot. Beating that illness and being able to work again. I absolutely love what I do. I was given a gift, and I'm a thankful man, and I try to respect and hone it and work on it, help it, and know it. That's how I try to pay the Good Lord back."

Andy also knew he owed Cindi as well. In 1990, he had this to say about his wife: "My happiness with Cindi has been a very steadying influence. Here's a young woman who was married to me less than (two months) when one morning I woke up damn near finished... I was without physical and emotional strength. But I found strength in my wife.... We'd put up our house for sale. We were going to move for good to North Carolina. But my wife realized, and I did, too, that if we moved, it would mean the end of my career. So we took the house off the market. I slowly got better and my determination came back. I wouldn't allow myself to fail, you see. I *hate* failure."

Linda Purl, cast as Matlock's daughter and partner Charlene,

124

had walked after the first season saying she was being underutilized. Hargrove agreed: "We discovered as time went on that it was very difficult to find the right line for her—whether she should be more of a daughter than an attorney, or vice versa."

The show's creators added three new additional female characters to make up for the departed Purl, but soon learned that audiences were watching for Andy. Try as they might, *Matlock* was not going to work as an ensemble show.

As the series progressed, and Griffith began to become more involved with the writing of plots and storylines, viewers began to see less of Matlock in court and more of the attorney at home or in other situations.

The first major change in the formula occurred during the two-hour opening episode of the 1989 season, "The Hunting Party." Andy spearheaded a special treat for himself, and for his friends in the historic village of Manteo by flying *Matlock* producers down to scout out the area.

Andy was more than excited about this on-location shoot. He was ecstatic. His fellow producers on the show knew this would make Andy a happy man, and besides, it offered an irresistible hook for publicity. From July 17 to August 4, film crews maneuvered around Roanoke Island on a daily basis with truckloads of cameras, lights, props and equipment.

"(Manteo) is very meaningful to me," Andy said at the time. "This is where I became an entertainer.... I don't have any really strong ties... to anywhere except here."

"He loved the show so much he brought it home," said supervising producer Jeff Peters while the episode was being shot. "Andy puts himself totally into this, especially in this episode. These are his people and his friends.... He's got this tremendous following. He's one of those stars who have endured and endeared."

About 20 locals were hired for the crews and dozens appeared on-screen as extras in the cast. Roughly a thousand people showed up to watch the final closing scene, which was set outside the 1904 Manteo Courthouse from which Ben Matlock emerged triumphant after winning yet another case.

Andy took pains to show off the beauty of the area, with beach scenes filmed in Nags Head, while other scenes featured the Waterside Theatre, Weir Point, the Manteo Waterfront and the Elizabethan Gardens.

"Two or three times a year, you see (Andy) in town, in the hardware store. To him, I think this is home. He's never lost touch," said Saint Clair Basnight Jr., whose family has been friends with Griffith since the late 1940s.

The filming of the episode pumped hundreds of thousands of dollars into the local economy, and Andy made sure the name Manteo was featured prominently in signs and on police cars. This free advertising was a great boon for a community that lives on tourism.

"Whatever you want to say about it, (*Matlock*) was number 15 for (1988) last year," Andy told a local reporter. "That's a lot of people to see the name 'Manteo' and to hear it pronounced correctly. Also, the people of the community are displayed in a good light. They are not made to look foolish or evil or anything negative."

Best of all, Andy made sure there was a role for his old friend R.G. "Bob" Armstrong, giving him a guest-starring role as Manteo Sheriff Dalton Parkes. This was a chance for Armstrong, who now lived in California, to return and relive his memories of Manteo and time spent with Griffith in *The Lost Colony*.

Andy also knew that once the camera crews were gone and another season of *Matlock* had been filmed, he and Cindi would be able to return to the solitude of Roanoke Island. On some days, a casual and barefoot Andy Griffith would drive into Manteo in his old restored "Woodie" station wagon to buy vegetables from the vendor downtown... and be able to return home at peace.

In late 1989, Andy received a call from his old friend and banjo playing cohort Lee Greenway, longtime makeup man for *The Andy Griffith Show*. Greenway, now retired, was living in Rutherfordton, North Carolina, where he had become a confidant for Francis Bavier. Bavier (also retired) had moved to Siler City in North Carolina in the early 1970s. The reclusive actress had been ailing for sometime, and now she wanted to speak to Andy one last time.

"... I called her and said, 'Hello, Francis.' And she said, 'Oh, Andy.' Her voice sounded very chipper. I said, 'Francis, is there... ' And she said, 'No, there's nothing you can do.... I must be made of cast iron. I had a heart attack and now I have cancer. And I am dying and I just wanted to say good-bye to you.' We had a beautiful conversation. That's the last time I talked to her," Griffith said in 1993.

October 3, 1992. Andy Griffith was on-stage in a huge outdoor theatre at Florida's Disney World. A heavy rain was falling, but the gathered audience paid the weather no mind. Their attention was on Andy, who was there to be inducted into the Academy of Television Arts and Science Hall of Fame.

With Griffith was Sheldon Leonard, and as part of the elaborate ceremony, many of their compatriots from *The Andy Griffith Show* were on-stage to pay tribute, including Aaron Ruben, Earle Hagen, Don Knotts and George Lindsey.

The day had been declared "Andy Griffith Day" in Florida, and at the public presentation prior to the actual awards ceremony Griffith expressed appreciation, as always, to "the best comedy writers in town." He closed by adding, "It was the best eight years professionally and personally of my entire life and I thank you very much."

Later that night, at the formal ceremony, Knotts and Lindsey made the official presentation to Andy with these words:

"For a career that reflects so deeply the actor's art on a canvas that you continue to fill with truth and integrity of character; and for your belief that humor can be found in the most unlikely places; and for insisting that television is a place for telling stories of love and human values that endure, we are proud to induct you, Andy Griffith, into the Television Academy Hall Of Fame."

A moved Griffith accepted with his trademark "I appreciate it." Afterward, he mused on his career:

"I suppose that when we film the last *Matlock* it's reasonable to assume that my career might be over, but I can't see it that way. It came too hard to give up easy. There were times in my life when I was sure I would not make it as an actor.... In acting, every career is many careers. There are a lot of failures and many long, dry spells when you cannot get work. When that happens, you have to keep telling yourself you will make a comeback.

"After *The Andy Griffith Show* ended, I could not get a part for a long time. I tried everywhere, but they all told me, 'You're not Andy Griffith. You're Andy Taylor. We don't need Andy Taylor.' So I could get only the role of a heavy. I became known as a heavy. I had to prove again that I was an actor.

"Still, I took what I could get, because I cannot live without acting. It's my life. Even today I watch the old Mayberry shows. I watch them while I have dinner. Each one is part of my life. I cannot forget them. They are real to me, something that really happened."

1992 also saw Capitol Records release a "Best Of" compilation culled from Andy's old comedy albums called *Andy Griffith: American Originals*. In an interview promoting the compact disc (the first Griffith record to receive the CD treatment), Andy was pleased with the re-release:

"I am very glad because I've gotten hundreds of thousands of letters from people asking about the recordings. It's kind of like a time capsule in that my style has changed so much. I don't think I'll ever have a record again."

In the fall of 1992, Andy settled into a seventh season of *Matlock*, but production moved from Los Angeles to Wilmington, North Carolina and the change in locale made a big difference. He and Cindi were able to commute by plane from work to Roanoke Island:

"I'd go home for three-day weekends, and whenever I got a week off from shooting. But Cindi and I are enjoying Wilmington so much—we've got a nice rented house—that I think we'll be staying put a lot... there are my kind of people here. I have a North Carolina (driver's) license and all our plates are North Carolina. The only thing we have in California now is an agent and a business manager."

He also noted that "I've got to quit saying I'm not going to do the series anymore. I've done that for the last three years and, well, I've got to quit singing the blues. I'm staying with the show and when the time comes that *Matlock* ends, I'll just find me something else."

Interestingly enough, along with the change of locale came a change of networks from NBC to ABC. Griffith believes the switch happened because Brandon Tartikoff, president of NBC Entertainment and staunch *Matlock* champion, left the network. Tartikoff had asked Andy to come back for another year, but after his departure, *Matlock* was suddenly not on the schedule.

Matlock did appear as an NBC mid-season replacement and go on for a complete sixth season. After that, Tartikoff's successor Warren Littlefield had a new deal for Andy. He offered to do six two-hour *Matlock* movies in one year... but the movies were to be parceled out and shown over the next three years. NBC was striving hard to push new shows for a younger audience, and the aging Griffith was not part of the image Littlefield had in mind.

"I don't think Warren Littlefield ever liked the show," Andy noted with grim amusement. "Or me that much."

Instead, Griffith's partner in the production of *Matlock*, Fred Silverman, put together a counter-proposal. Silverman's package included the addition of new characters... coupled with the cost-saving idea of allowing the show to be produced in North Carolina—long a growing arena for Hollywood movie productions. Andy was willing, but the next thing he knew the trade papers were announcing that NBC had canceled the series.

Not to worry. Within 24 hours, ABC expressed a desire to bring the show over to their network, where the ratings have continued to hold steady. Plus, Griffith and company were much happier to be with an outfit that wanted them around.

"And I'm just too old to be canceled, so I was thrilled," Griffith observed.

Another *Matlock* producer, Joel Steiger, believes Griffith's personal following was a major reason *Matlock* survived the network switch successfully: "He has this enormous following of people who will follow him no matter what network he's on."

In late 1992, a deal was struck to produce *The Andy Griffith Show Reunion*. Griffith wasn't ready to undertake this type of retrospective due to the seven days a week spent working on *Matlock*, but, as he remembered in a lengthy interview given to *The Charlotte Observer*:

"... I didn't make that clear to an agent there at the William Morris Agency.... And I had to do it, because I had to be sure that the people who were doing it did it right. Everybody thinks they know about the Griffith show, but they don't. And it's much more complicated than people think."

After Andy helped choose clips and excerpts from the series, he took a day off from *Matlock's* shooting schedule to film the special. Ron Howard, Don Knotts, Jim Nabors, George Lindsey and Jack Dodson were flown into the Carolco studios in Wilmington, where a backdrop reminiscent of the Mayberry Courthouse had been constructed not far from the standing *Matlock* set.

And then, the old friends proceeded to spend the day talking and laughing and playing to the camera, making up some of what they said as they went along, and reading set-ups and transitions provided from a script written partly by an uncredited Andy Griffith himself.

As for how the show holds up for Andy today?

"Oh, it's a big change," he said in response to a query about the difference between the black and white and the later color episodes. "The black and white shows were better... It comes on about supper time here (in Manteo), and sometimes Cindi and I will watch an episode if we particularly liked it and laugh out loud. And if it's one I didn't really care for, I wouldn't watch it."

Andy and Ron Howard in 1986

c✿✐⊙✐✿⊃

In 1993 Griffith noted he never has lost the fear that every actor shares—the fear that each assignment will be his last. With his long career in the industry and enormous success in television, most would think Andy's worries to be unfounded, but he still remembers the fallow period he endured during the 1970s:

"I've only had two successful shows (*The Andy Griffith Show* and *Matlock*). Besides those, there was *Salvage-1*, which only lasted a year. There was a real turkey called *Headmaster*, which I think went 13-14 segments. And there was *The New Andy Griffith Show*— I only did about ten of those. I also did innumerable single shots and pilots, and I even did one of those 20-minute wonders called 'series presentations' for a network.

"Doing a one-hour series is real hard work and I don't know that I want to do that on a regular basis. To tell you the truth, I would rather be just a regular actor who goes up for parts (in movies or as a guest on other projects) and gets 'em or doesn't get 'em. That's what I'd rather be."

As *Matlock* continued, more of Griffith's personal preferences started to shine through, including an increased reliance on comedy. A story supervisor and executive producer in addition to being the star, Andy maintains the habits established during his years on *The Andy Griffith Show* and keeps a close eye on *Matlock* scripts—which may explain the show's enduring success.

After all, Griffith knows what his audience wants, and more often than not, it's the same thing he enjoys:

"I make comments on (the story outline), and then a script is written—and we all work on that. A lot of producers don't like for actors to be writers, but Joel (Steiger) doesn't object and I do love it. Sometimes the writers make Matlock too serious. Matlock is a very bright man, but he's vain.... When the others make him too serious, I talk it out of the script while they're filming. I play against the lines. But it works, because I think I'm a decent writer."

Andy on Matlock from 1994:

"(Matlock) has real feet of clay.... This character is very cheap, cheap in every way.... He thinks he looks great in these gray suits. He thinks he has a wonderful figure. It's fun for me. I'm not a lawyer. I'm not all that bright. I *know* what kind of figure I've got and I'm not vain. I'm also not cheap. But I really love to play this part and allow this character to have all these weaknesses."

For *Matlock's* eighth season, Griffith was surprised when ABC wanted more shows to broadcast during the 1993-1994 season:

"I told (ABC) to give me a couple of weeks to think about it. I wanted to talk to the producer, to see if we could do some different kinds of shows—and we are—about human values, and stories with more comedy... Mystery shows are always three-suspect or formula shows, and I've been trying to get around that for years. If we get a story that's straight mystery, I'll find a place to put in some comedy—I can't live without it."

When the deal was struck, Griffith stood by his decision to lighten the tone of the series:

"As far as I'm concerned, I don't care about the mystery. I know I have to do the courtroom scene. I look at that as a little short play and prepare it as such. The comedy is what I'm primarily interested in, that's what I spend most of my time on."

However, if and when Andy does decide that Matlock has defended his last case, he has no intention of settling down. If a suitable partner can be found, he'd like to do some writing and one imagines he'll stay involved in acting. Much like his habits on *The Andy Griffith Show*, Andy remains focused on whatever project is occupying his attention.

"It's hard for me to consider anything else while I'm doing (*Matlock*), Andy said in 1993. "I have a very one-track mind. Sometimes at home I get upset with myself because I won't be able to find things... Yet when it comes to work, I know exactly what I'm doing. I know where everybody is standing. I know every detail of what I'm doing. Cindi says that's why I am able to have that concentration, because I'm able to let it go everywhere else."

Andy has decided *Matlock* will be his last television series. The rigors of doing an hour-long drama for over a decade have been exhausting, and to even think of attempting another half-hour comedy or sitcom makes Griffith weary:

"It's too hard nowadays. I'm not interested in doing a multicamera show with an audience. Because that requires a different kind of writing than I'm used to, and they can't afford to do a half-hour comedy with one camera. That's the way the old Griffith show was shot... I am hoping to do television movies. There's nothing wrong with that, if it's good."

He would like to do a feature film with Ron Howard, if the right script came along. "Ronny's very busy, but he and I keep each other in the back of our heads. I care very much about him."

In a 1994 interview with William Friday, Andy jokingly said:

"... I hope to work as an actor as long as I can remember my lines. You know, guys my age, they're dying out and there's always a place for you."

Andy's continuing success and popularity has kept demand high for public appearances, which he turns down as a rule:

"I used to do a lot of that stuff, but it's just too hard... I elected some years ago not to make appearances anymore. I'll tell you why: It's like George Burns says. 'They only want you to do five minutes. Well, it only takes about two weeks to put together a good five minutes.' Comedy, as they say, ain't easy."

Griffith has avoided attending the yearly conventions dedicated to *The Andy Griffith Show* for the same reason. His performance schedule for the last decade has been taken up by *Matlock*, and he has always preferred to spend his free time on Roanoke Island. When Andy does agree to make the rare public appearance, it can be guaranteed he will be ready. Andy is always prepared, but the preparation takes time:

"I appreciate that they have these rerun watcher clubs. I appreciate that and I appreciate people do that. But... I can't go down to somewhere and be a part of some sloppy show... I can't just get out there and 'aw, shucks' myself. That ain't entertainment.... And I would be very disappointed and I would be deceiving the audience if I go on in and just show up."

In late 1994, after the popularity of a slew of motion pictures based on classic television shows, Hollywood came knocking on Mayberry's door and wanted to buy the rights to turn *The Andy Griffith Show* into a big-budget film with a new cast. Andy was interested. After all, between the reunion movie and the CBS retrospective, he had gone back to Mayberry twice himself.

But the deal was withdrawn when Andy asked for one important concession:

"They wouldn't give me script approval. The old Griffith show means a great deal to me and I don't want to kill its memory. I'm not saying they couldn't have done a wonderful job with it. But I'm afraid."

Fans everywhere understood. Recreating Mayberry's magic with new actors is a feat beyond even Hollywood's capabilities.

When asked about another Mayberry reunion movie, Griffith responded, "I don't think so. Jack (Dodson) is gone. Hal Smith is gone. Howard McNear is gone. Ronny Howard has a big movie career going. That leaves Don and me, and you put us side by side and it looks like we were both let out of the home for an hour."

In a first-person account Andy gave to Lillian and Helen Ross for *The Player* in the early 1960s, he stated:

"I'm not in the entertainment business to make money. I've never particularly cared one way or the other about that. I came from a poor background. I was happy as a child. I was happy as a teenager. I was happy as a young adult. I never had capital, but I was never unhappy because of that. When I discovered I could entertain, I worked hard at it. It's the only thing I do well. I can't be a company director, I can't be an accountant, I can't make furniture, but I *can* entertain."

And as for retirement... ?

"My God, give me a break—retire and you start to die," a more mature Andy once said.

Matlock

FILMOGRAPHY

Theatrical

A Face In The Crowd 1957. Director: Elia Kazan. Writer: Budd Schulberg. Songs written by Tom Glazer and Budd Schulberg. Black and white. Released by Warner Bros.

In his motion picture debut, Griffith stars with Patricia Neal, Walter Matthau, Anthony Franciosa, Rip Torn and Lee Remick (also her first film).

Griffith has the lead role as Lonesome Rhodes, a homespun philosopher, country musician and television demagogue. As Marcia Jefferies, Neal discovers Rhodes in a county jail when he's practicing his trade as a hillbilly singer and turns him first into a radio star, and later into a popular television personality with his own live show. Rhodes soon becomes crazed with power, gleefully hawking "Vitajex," (a product he knows doesn't work) to please his sponsors and bragging about how the masses love him.

Rhodes becomes a national figure, and as his influence grows (Rhodes has political aspirations), Marcia discovers her creation's darker side. She loves him, but knows she has to put an end to Lonesome's reign of the airwaves before anyone else can be hurt. Marcia figuratively pulls the plug on Rhodes by exposing him for what he is on live television... leaving him powerless and alone.

Critical reaction to Andy's performance at the time was almost universal in praising the actor. In his 1993 book *Alternate Oscars*, author and film critic Danny Peary believed that Griffith should have won an Oscar for Best Actor in 1957 for his work in *A Face In The Crowd.* Of course, newcomer Griffith wasn't even nominated and the award went to Sir Alec Guinness for his role as Colonel Nicholson in *The Bridge On The River Kwai.*

Peary had this to say about Andy's performance:

"For Griffith fans who saw (*No Time For Sergeants*), or who got used to his easygoing country sheriff in the long-running *The Andy Griffith Show*, Lonesome Rhodes is quite a shock, a perversion of the other two characters (and of the naive Griffith of comedy albums).... The North Carolina-born Griffith studied to be a preacher, and that's evident in this volcanic performance, where Lonesome continually takes center stage and, with unbridled energy and the right mix of superiority and humility, attempts to convince everyone around him that he is right.... The monster out of his system, Griffith would never play such a high-strung, explosive character again... it's almost too bad, because he was capable of playing a villain different from all others who appeared in the cinema."

Cue Magazine noted, "It is probably the best actor's performance of this year," about Griffith's work in the film, which is now housed in the National Archives.

No Time For Sergeants 1958. Director: Mervyn Leroy. Writer: John Lee Mahin. Based on the novel by Mac Hyman and the Broadway play by Ira Levin. Black and white. Released by Warner Bros.

Stars Griffith, Nick Adams, Myron McCormick, Murray Hamilton and Don Knotts.

The Broadway hit was brought to the silver screen in a funny and well-handled translation, with key cast members Griffith and McCormick returning in the Will Stockdale and Sergeant King roles. Even Don Knotts made the transition in his small, yet memorable role as Manual Dexterity Corporal, but a young Nick Adams replaced Roddy McDowell as Stockdale's long suffering pal Ben.

The screenplay for the film utilized both Mac Hyman's original novel, as well as the play adaptation by Ira Levin, keeping basically the same structure and many of the same gags. A box-office smash, *Sergeants* took in somewhere between $7,500,000 and $9,000,000 in domestic rentals for Warner Brothers and was ranked as the fourth top picture of 1958—making it the most financially successful of any of Griffith's films.

Critic Bosley Crowther noted that "(*Sergeants*) has the same marvelous Andy Griffith, who created Will on the stage... (and) as Will, he should not only win new friends but also establish the character so firmly that the memory of it will be indelible. We strongly suspect that Mr. Griffith will have a hard time shedding himself of the aura of Will... with his sunny, smiling face and Southern drawl."

Onionhead 1958. Director: Norman Taurog. Writer: Nelson Gidding. Based on a best-selling novel by Weldon Hill. Color. Released by Warner Bros.

Stars Griffith, Felicia Farr, Walter Matthau, Erin O'Brien and Joey Bishop.

In a calculated follow-up to *No Time For Sergeants*, *Onionhead* features Andy as Al Woods, a sad-sack Coast Guard cook stationed on the U.S.S. Periwinkle. After a failed college love affair, Woods joins the Coast Guard and finds himself surrounded by wacky shipmates, a tigress of a new love interest, a battle with a submarine where he becomes a hero, and a climactic naval inquiry. An uneven mix of comedy, romance, intrigue and action that never quite jells on screen, *Onionhead* was not received well by critics or the public.

Critic A. H. Weiler said, "As might be expected, Mr. Griffith is outstanding in the role of the gentle, but basically tough and calculating country boy who is not nearly the rube he was in his previous stint in the celluloid 'armed forces.' Although the comic moments are not regular occurrences in *Onionhead*, both Mr. Griffith and Walter Matthau... succeed in making a few of them (one drunk scene is specially recommended) howlingly funny.... (But) in *Onionhead*, however, their course is only occasionally clear and memorable."

The Second Time Around 1961. Director: Vincent Sherman. Writers: Oscar Saul and Cecil Dan Hansen. Color. Released by MGM.

Stars Griffith, Debbie Reynolds, Steve Forrest and Thelma Ritter.

Farfetched western comedy with a complicated plot set in Arizona around 1910. Eastern city slicker and widow Debbie Reynolds becomes sheriff of a frontier western town with the help of the film's two heroic leading men, Pat Collins (Andy) and Dan Jones (Steve Forrest). A slapstick romance filmed in CinemaScope, the movie looks good... even when the story becomes ridiculous. Debbie chooses Steve to be her romantic interest, but as one critic at the time noted, "The audience will choose Griffith because he provided a little seasoning and all the laughs."

Andy commented in 1962: "In Debbie's picture I just change costumes. Otherwise, I'm the same as I am on TV."

Angel In My Pocket 1969. Director: Alan Rafkin. Writers: Jim Fritzell and Everett Greenbaum. Color. Released by Universal Studios.

Stars Griffith, Jerry Van Dyke, Lee Meriwether, Gary Collins, Edgar Buchanan, Kay Medford and Jack Dodson.

Griffith returns to feature films with a G-rated family comedy. He plays Sam Whitehead, a small town minister trying to keep the peace between two warring factions of his congregation, a local mayoralty campaign, and his own wife and kids. The gags come fast and furious (as to be expected from *Andy Griffith Show* writers

Fritzell and Greenbaum), including a funny bit where Reverend Andy finds an organ for the church courtesy of a burlesque theatre. Unfortunately, with mixed reviews and audience apathy, *Angel* did not generate ticket sales and Griffith would not make another motion picture for six more years.

Hearts Of The West 1975. Director: Howard Zieff. Writer: Rob Thompson. Color. Released by MGM.

Stars Griffith, Jeff Bridges, Blythe Danner, Donald Pleasence and Alan Arkin.

A rambling, easy-going period piece set in the early 1930s, *Hearts* tells the story of how would-be western pulp writer Lewis Tater (Jeff Bridges), a Depression-era Iowa hick, ends up stranded in Los Angeles after coming out west to enroll at a bogus writing school. To eat, Tater joins up as a movie extra with "Tumbleweed Productions," a cheap film company cranking out formulaic horse operas.

Andy co-stars as Howard Pike, Tater's mentor in the Hollywood stunt work business. Griffith effortlessly steals the show in this little film that did not do well during its original release, but did find a home on the college film circuit. As one reviewer noted: "Once every so often, Griffith gets a role that reminds us how good he really is."

Rustler's Rhapsody 1985. Director: Hugh Wilson. Writer: Hugh Wilson. Color. Released by Paramount Pictures.

Stars Griffith, Tom Berenger, G.W. Bailey and Marilu Henner.

. A clever spoof of "B" westerns that is enjoyable while never taking itself very seriously, *Rustler's Rhapsody* features the adventures of our smiling, two-fisted hero, Rex O'Herlihan—a singing

142

cowboy. The film is deadpan and funny in how it celebrates such traditional western clichés as the drunken sidekick, the town prostitute and "Wildflower," the dancing palomino.

Griffith has a supporting role as bad guy Colonel Ticonderoga, a rich and effeminate cattle baron with an aching desire for his ranch hands. Director and writer Wilson is best known for creating television's *WKRP In Cincinnati*, and he brings the same masterful control from the show's ensemble cast to this film.

Made-For-Television

The Strangers In 7-A November 14, 1972. CBS. Andy and actress Ida Lupino star as Artie and Iris Sawyer, a New York couple who become hostages in their own apartment—held captive by a sadistic would-be bank robber and his gang of young thieves. With Michael Brandon, James A. Watson, Jr. and Tim McIntire.

Pray For The Wildcats January 23, 1973. ABC. Evil businessman Sam Farragut (Andy) challenges three advertising executives to a wild motorcycle race down the California Baja peninsula and into Mexico... with his lucrative advertising account as bait. The film also starred three other familiar faces from series television: Robert Reed, Marjoe Gortner and William Shatner.

Go Ask Alice January 24, 1973. ABC. The agonized and dramatic life story of a teen-age drug addict. Filmed in a documentary style and based on the actual diary of a 16-year-old girl who, with the help of her family and friends, tried to find her way back to the real world after an overdose of LSD. Andy was cast in a supporting role as Priest. With Jamie Smith-Jackson and William Shatner.

Winter Kill April 15, 1974 ABC. A suspense thriller where sheriff Sam Adams (Andy) investigates a series of murders in the small winter resort town of Eagle Lake, California. A pilot for the short-lived television series *Adams Of Eagle Lake*. With Sherri North.

Savages September 11, 1974. ABC. Griffith stars as Horton Maddock, a wealthy New York attorney enjoying a western hunting trip... until he accidentally kills an old prospector. Now, to protect his reputation, the attorney must stalk and cold-bloodedly murder his own guide before he can return to being "civilized." With Sam Bottoms, Noah Beery, Jr. and James Best.

Street Killing September 12, 1976. ABC. Andy gets in some pre-*Matlock* practice in the courtroom as Gus Brenner, a prosecuting attorney for the New York City District Attorney's Office. Brenner becomes determined to nail a gangland figure who has made a deliberate murder look like a racial mugging—and connects the crime to a crooked politician. With Bradford Dillman, Harry Guardino and Robert Loggia.

Six Characters In Search Of An Author 1976/1977. A PBS/ Hollywood Television Theatre production of the famous play by Pirandello. Andy was the "Husband-Father."

Andy comments in 1986: "... I found the producers had picked me 'cause they knew I'd play (the character) as 'Everyman'—as the possibility for any man's life instead of doing it like a classic. Except for a long time I didn't understand the character and had trouble playing him as much of anything. Then, one night I drove past the house where I'd lived for many years with my first wife.

"I was divorced (at the time). And I was playing this character who'd sent his wife away, thinking that he'd have his youth over again. He'd do all sorts of things he hadn't had a chance to do when he was younger. And there'd be women all over the place, see. Well, that doesn't happen in the play. As it doesn't happen in real life. I'd thought, too, oh boy, I'm a single man now and things are really gonna *happen*...

"They didn't. And when I saw that house that night I *knew* that character. "Cause even though the circumstances had changed, he was still the same man he was before—and so was I."

The Girl In The Empty Grave September 20, 1977. NBC. Andy stars as Police Chief Abel Marsh of Jasper Lake, California, who finds himself investigating the mysterious return of a young woman who supposedly died in an automobile accident a year before. An interesting mix of humor and suspense, the film features a colorful cast of small town deputies and townspeople.

Andy is well cast as Marsh and handles the changes from comedy to drama adeptly in this, the first of two Abel Marsh TV movies that served as tryouts for an unproduced series. Griffith had high hopes for this radical combination of "Mayberry" and murder mystery ("If we should get on and if we should last a little while, then I think we can come up with something that is unusual for television.") Originally called *Abel*. With Jonathan Banks, Mitzi Hoag, George Gaynes and Sharon Spelman.

Deadly Game December 3, 1977. NBC. Abel Marsh returns in the second of two pilot movies. This time the mystery involves a covert U.S. military tanker truck containing a lethal biological weapon of life-destroying chemicals... and the aftermath when the truck is overturned in Jasper Lake. Both films were executive produced by Richard O. Linke for MGM and Andy's own Manteo Productions. With Dan O'Herlihy, Morgan Woodward and Sharon Spelman.

Salvage-1 January 20, 1979. ABC. Two-hour TV movie that served as a pilot for the television series. The film introduced the premise of junkman supreme Harry Broderick (Griffith) and his quest to salvage millions of dollars of discarded space equipment left behind by NASA on the moon. With Joel Higgins, Trish Stewart, Richard Jaeckel and J. Jay Saunders. Their first mission a success, the crew went on to other impossible salvage operations in the series including the towing of an iceberg and the rescue of the Skylab space station.

For Lovers Only October 15, 1982. ABC. The setting is a honeymoon haven in the Poconos run by founder/owner Vernon Bliss, better known to viewing audiences as Andy Griffith. Designed as a potential pilot for a weekly comedy series, the film was pitched as "a land-locked *Love Boat*." If sold, it would have been known as *Honeymoon Hotel*. With Deborah Raffin, Gordon Jump, Katherine Helmond, Sally Kellerman and Gary Sandy.

Murder In Coweta County February 15, 1983. CBS. Andy is paired with Johnny Cash in this fact-based suspense thriller about "The Kingdom," a backwoods Georgia dynasty of illegal moonshine in 1948. Cash is the good guy, Sheriff Lamar Potts. Griffith is the heavy, John Wallace. Sheriff Potts wants Wallace for the killing of a poor black tenant farmer... and is determined to bring him in. With Earl Hindman as J.H. Potts and June Carter Cash as Mayhayley Lancaster, an eccentric old soothsayer.

The Demon Murder Case March 6, 1983. NBC. Demonic possession set in a New England town. Loosely based on a true story where the defendant literally claimed that "the devil made him do it." Andy is Guy Harris, a "demonologist" who teams with psychic Cloris Leachman and priest Eddie Albert to exorcise the young man. Also starring Ken Kercheval, Joyce Van Patten, Kevin Bacon and Harvey Fierstein as the voice of the demon.

Crimes Of Innocence October 27, 1985. NBC. Inspired by actual events, this drama features Griffith in the role of Judge Julius Spencer, a harsh and unsympathetic figure who believes in only the most severe punishments for the teenagers who come through his courtroom. Spencer's downfall occurs after he sends a young girl to an adult jail, where she is raped and brutalized. With Diane Ladd, Shawnee Smith, Ralph Waite and Brent Spiner.

Diary Of A Perfect Murder March 3, 1986. NBC. A highly rated TV movie featuring the first appearance of Atlanta-based lawyer Ben Matlock, a brilliant Harvard-educated attorney in the mold of Perry Mason. Griffith shines in what was to become yet another signature role. In this thinly-disguised pilot for the *Matlock* series, the lawyer is called upon to defend a top television journalist accused of murdering his ex-wife, a prominent Atlanta news anchorwoman. With Lori Lethin as Charlene Matlock (a role played by Linda Purl in the series) and Kene Holiday as Tyler Hudson, Matlock's legman and private investigator.

Return To Mayberry   April 13, 1986. NBC. One of the few TV reunion movies to actually work, *Return To Mayberry* was the highest rated television movie for 1986. The reunion of 15 of the original cast members from *The Andy Griffith Show* with two of the show's best writers (Harvey Bullock and Everett Greenbaum), and original director Bob Sweeney made for a return that was true in spirit and execution to the series. Even composer Earle Hagen was coaxed out of retirement to write the score.

Andy and Helen Taylor come back from Cleveland to Mayberry, where Andy intends to run for sheriff again. However, complications ensue when he finds Deputy Barney Fife has also entered the race. Plus, Andy has to deal with delivering his newborn grandson, Opie's decision to leave Mayberry for the big city, the usual escapades of Ernest T. Bass, and a monster living in Myer's Lake.

However, by the movie's end, many of the loose ends left from the original series have been given closure. Barney and Thelma Lou finally marry. Andy is re-elected sheriff. Opie does indeed flee the nest of home. The death of Aunt Bee is gently addressed (but oddly, no mention is made of Floyd).

As the credits roll, everything is put right in Mayberry once more.

Some filmed scenes were later cut from the movie, including Gomer singing "Because" at Barney and Thelma Lou's wedding, and a brief bit with county clerk Howard showing off his new girl, Rose, a librarian from Mt. Pilot.

147

With Griffith, Don Knotts, Ron Howard, Jim Nabors, George Lindsey, Aneta Corsaut, Betty Lynn, Hal Smith, Jack Dodson, Howard Morris, Maggie Peterson-Mancuso, Denver Pyle and the Dillards.

Under The Influence September 28, 1986. CBS. Andy stars as Noah Talbot, an aging father with four children in the small town where he and his wife have lived for over 30 years. Talbot runs a hardware store and presents a smiling face to his customers, but his family knows differently. Noah is an alcoholic and his binges are becoming more frequent and violent. Finally, after Noah's drinking puts him in the hospital, his wife acknowledges that something must be done about his disease before it rips the family apart. With Joyce Van Patten, Paul Provenza and Keanu Reeves.

The Gift Of Love September 25, 1994. CBS. A weepy, but well-acted melodrama with Griffith as Phil Doucet, a retiree who suffers a deadly heart attack and recovers, only to find his bypass surgery is failing. Without a donor heart he doesn't have long to live. However, fate intervenes and Doucet ends up with his beloved grandson's heart as a transplant after the boy dies in an accident. Between this life-affirming event and a later encounter with a 17-year-old runaway (Olivia Burnette), Doucet manages to heal the rift between himself and his estranged daughter (Blair Brown). Originally called *Set For Life*.

Griffith was quoted as saying he "liked (*The Gift Of Love*) very much.... It's about love, for one thing, and I liked it because of that. I thought it was well written and I felt I could play it.... I told Blair Brown after we read the script on the first day that she was the best actress I had worked with in a long, long time. This... has some moments that are very powerful, and it's very well put together."

TELEVISION SERIES

The Andy Griffith Show October 3, 1960/September 16, 1968. 249 Episodes. CBS. One of the all-time classic television shows with a cast of now-household names, including Griffith as Sheriff Andy Taylor, Don Knotts as Deputy Barney Fife, Francis Bavier as Aunt Bee, Ron Howard as Opie Taylor, Jim Nabors as Gomer Pyle, George Lindsey as Goober Pyle, Hal Smith as Otis Campbell, Howard McNear as Floyd Lawson, Aneta Corsaut as Helen Crump, Betty Lynn as Thelma Lou, Jack Dodson as Howard Sprague and Howard Morris as Ernest T. Bass.

The Andy Griffith Show officially went off the air in 1968. However, through syndication, the show continues to attract fans of all ages and backgrounds, and remains as popular today as during its original top ten run.

Set in a timeless pocket of North Carolina, the world of Mayberry allows viewers to visit an era when residents didn't have to lock their doors and windows, children could walk the streets without worry and not fear talking to strangers, neighbors were neighborly and people cared about their fellow man.

There was no crime to speak of, except for colorful moonshiners and a giggling man-child throwing rocks. The sheriff didn't even wear a gun. He was father to his son, his deputy, and pretty much to the entire town.

Producer Sheldon Leonard once referred to Mayberry as the real star of the show, and in many ways he was correct. When you enter the town of Mayberry, you experience the love of family— related or not; the warmth of a kindly aunt who spreads useful advice with slices of freshly baked apple pie; and the treasure of a true friend, who, despite his ineptitude, always means to do his best.

Mayberry, R.F.D. September 23, 1968/September 6, 1971. 78 Episodes. CBS. After Griffith left *The Andy Griffith Show*, the series continued for three more seasons under this new name, with Aunt Bee, Goober Pyle, Howard Sprague and Emmett the Fix-It Man remaining in Mayberry. In Andy's absence they were joined by Ken Berry as new male lead, Sam Jones, who coincidentally was also a widower with a young son. Sam's steady girl was Millie Swanson (Arlene Golonka).

Griffith made infrequent guest appearances, marrying Helen Crump and leaving town for a new job up north as a postal inspector in the very first episode. But the eye of Andy wasn't far since he and Richard O. Linke both served as Executive Producers of the series. When canceled by CBS in 1971 as part of a network-wide attempt to rid itself of a "rural" image, the show was still in the top ten. After the cancellation, Griffith said, "when *Mayberry R.F.D.* was canceled it was as if a very important member of my family had died. I mourned it for years."

Headmaster September 18, 1970/January 1, 1971. 13 Episodes. CBS. Griffith starred as Andy Thompson, the Headmaster of the private Concord Prep School in this half hour drama series with comedic overtones. An early example of the "dramedy," the show focused on the personal problems of the students and Andy's homelife. His wife Margaret, played by Claudette Nevins, was one of the school's English teachers and his best friend, physical education teacher (and comedy relief) Jerry Brownell was brought to life by sitcom mainstay Jerry Van Dyke. The public was unwilling to accept Griffith in such a contemporary role so soon after Sheriff Andy Taylor, and in an effort to boost the show's ratings the format was changed in mid-season and retooled as *The New Andy Griffith Show*.

The New Andy Griffith Show January 8, 1971/May 21, 1971. 10 or 13 Episodes. CBS. From high school Headmaster to southern small town mayor, Griffith was now Andy Sawyer, overseer of Greenwood, North Carolina in a role much like his earlier success as Andy Taylor. Unfortunately, viewers weren't buying the "new" Andy, even with a complete cast and locale change. Without a strong comic foil such as Don Knotts (who did show up for the premiere as a guest star), the new format was soon canceled. With Lee Meriwether as Andy's wife, Lee, and Ann Morgan Guilbert as busybody sister-in-law Nora.

Great Roads Of America 1973. Syndicated. Andy served as narrator for this obscure half-hour documentary series, which focused on American highways and byways.

Adams Of Eagle Lake August 23 and 30, 1975. 2 Episodes. ABC. Andy stars as Sheriff Sam Adams, first seen in the TV movie/pilot *Winter Kill*. A police drama set in the resort town of Eagle Lake California, the project was executive produced by Richard O. Linke. With a young Nick Nolte as Jerry Troy.

Salvage-1 January 29, 1979/November 11, 1979. 15 Episodes and a two-hour TV movie pilot. ABC. An adventure series with Andy as Harry Broderick, a junk and scrap dealer interested in more than your average person's throwaways. Launched with a two hour TV movie that saw Griffith, along with co-stars Joel Higgins as Skip Carmichael (a former astronaut) and Trish Stewart as Melanie Sloza (a fuel expert) build their own rocket, christen it as "The Vulture" and fly to the moon to salvage the space equipment and debris left behind by NASA.

After the pilot, the crew went on to use their ingenuity and the Vulture to move an iceberg from the North Pole to a drought-stricken island, rid a haunted house of ghosts, find the missing link on a jungle isle and return to outer space to retrieve a satellite filled with gold components. Short-lived, but fanciful and fun with a wonderful Sousa-esque "oompah" musical score.

The Yeagers June 1 and 8, 1980. 2 Episodes and two-hour pilot. ABC. A mere blip on the prime time schedule, *The Yeagers* starred Andy as Carroll Yeager, the head of a family-run logging and mining company in Washington state. A widower with three sons and a daughter, Andy had his hands full as the family patriarch. Interestingly enough, in the pilot film *Trouble In High Timber County*, the Yeager character was played by character actor Eddie Albert. Even more confusing, the pilot wasn't shown until after the series had aired.

Matlock September 20, 1986/to present NBC/ABC. Launched with the two hour pilot film *Diary Of A Perfect Murder*. Original working series title, *The Firm*.

After a wide assortment of television movies, variety specials and failed TV pilots throughout the seventies, lightning strikes twice as Andy Griffith succeeds with a second top-rated series. Driven by the character of Benjamin L. Matlock, a disheveled but wily Atlanta lawyer who uses a combination of good ol' common sense and a keen legal brain to outwit his opponents in court, the series is one-part Perry Mason and one-part Andy Griffith.

Similar in feel to *Murder She Wrote*, Matlock is definitely a one-man show and Griffith is more than up to the task. The series was created and tailor-made for Griffith by *Columbo* and *The Man From U.N.C.L.E.* veteran Dean Hargrove, along with some help from executive producer Fred Silverman.

As the seasons pass, characters come and go as Matlock's associates, including Linda Purl as Charlene Matlock (daughter number one), Kene Holliday as Tyler Hudson (assistant number one), Nancy Stafford as Michelle Thomas (partner), Kari Lizer as Cassie Phillips (a law clerk), Clarence Gilyard, Jr. as Conrad McMasters (assistant number two), Julie Sommars as Julie March (an assistant district attorney), Don Knotts as Les "Ace" Calhoun (Matlock's next door neighbor), Brynn Thayer as Leanne McIntyre (daughter number two), Daniel Roebuck as Cliff Lewis (another attorney) and Warren Frost as Billy Lewis (Matlock's hometown nemesis).

However, no one seems to mind the shuffling of the supporting players since attention is always focused on the main man himself. As the years have passed, the series has shifted from being a straight murder mystery to a more lighthearted hour of comedy (with dramatic elements mixed in). Griffith has even made Matlock a musician, with many country-music performers appearing as guest stars.

ANTHOLOGIES/TV MINI-SERIES

The U.S. Steel Hour March 15, 1955. Andy's television debut as Will Stockdale in the first dramatization of Mac Hyman's *No Time For Sergeants*. The production was a first for its time—most live television plays were dramas, not comedies. Directed by Alex Segal. Adapted by Ira Levin. Produced by Segal and the Theatre Guild. With Harry Clark and Eddie Leroy.

Playhouse 90 March 13, 1958. Andy in *The Male Animal*. A little seen early effort that Andy dismissed as a "mistake." He was still apologizing four years later: "I hate to tell you just how terrible I was in that show."

Washington: Behind Closed Doors September 6, 1977/September 11, 1977. ABC. Six-part mini-series focusing on the President of the United States and his inner circle. Adapted from John Ehrlichman's novel *The Company*. Griffith portrayed Esker Anderson, the retiring president in this thinly disguised dramatization of the Watergate saga. With Jason Robards as President Richard Monckton and Cliff Robertson as William Martin.

Centennial October 1, 1978 to February 4, 1979. 12 Episodes. 26 hours. NBC. Shown over a five month period, *Centennial* was adapted from the sprawling James Michener novel tracing the growth of Colorado from 1756 to 1978 and stands as the longest mini-series ever attempted for television. Epic in structure, the series featured a sterling cast. Andy was featured as Professor Lewis Vernor, who researches the history of the town of Centennial.

Roots: The Next Generations February 18 to 23 and 25, 1979. ABC. Epic 14 hour sequel to *Roots*, that continued the saga of writer Alex Haley and his quest to discover his past. The series picked up where the first mini-series left off in 1882. A literal all-star cast was featured, including Georg Stanford Brown, Henry Fonda, Debbie Allen, Diahann Carroll, Marlon Brando and James Earl Jones as Haley. Andy appeared in the latter part of the series in the role of Commander Robert Munroe.

From Here To Eternity February 14, 21 and 28, 1979. NBC. Six hour mini-series based on the classic 1953 film and novel by James Jones. Using the extra running time to expand on the original story of military life in Hawaii on the eve of the attack on Pearl Harbor, the mini-series featured an all-star cast including Natalie Wood as Karen Holmes, William Devane as Sergeant Milt Warden, Kim Basinger as Lorene Rogers, Peter Boyle as Fatso Judson, Roy Thinnes as Captain Dana Holmes and Andy Griffith as General Barney Slater. A regular series using most of the same cast planned for the fall of 1979 never materialized.

Murder In Texas May 3 and 4, 1981. NBC. Andy shines as Ash Robinson, a father obsessed with bringing his daughter's killer to justice in this four-hour dramatization of the infamous late 1960s Texas murder case. The case involved a noted Houston plastic surgeon accused of murdering his first wife in order to marry another woman. One of the many fact-based murder mysteries Griffith would make during the 1980s and possibly the finest. Andy was nominated for an Emmy Award for his work in the film. With Farrah Fawcett, Katharine Ross, Barry Corbin, Bill Dana and Sam Elliott as Dr. John Hill.

A critic for *People Weekly* noted that *"Murder In Texas* is an often compelling four-hour melodrama about a sensational murder case.... The real show stealer, though, is Andy Griffith as Farrah (Fawcett's) vengeful millionaire oilman father."

Fatal Vision November 18 and 19, 1984. NBC. Based on the best-selling non-fiction book by Joe McGinniss, this two-part miniseries presents the story of Doctor Jeffrey MacDonald, a man accused of murdering his pregnant wife and two small daughters... and his father-in-law's crusade to bring MacDonald to justice. Although his screen time was brief, Griffith's work in the second half of the mini-series was seen by NBC Entertainment President Brandon Tartikoff... and led to the development of *Matlock* for Andy as a series vehicle.

John Leonard, a reviewer for *New York* magazine had this to say: "Andy Griffith, an underrated actor, has a bit part as Victor Worheide, the eccentric government prosecutor who is finally prevailed upon to go after MacDonald; he is denied the minutes and the nuance." With Karl Malden, Eva Marie Saint, Barry Newman and Gary Cole as MacDonald.

BROADWAY

No Time For Sergeants Opened October 20, 1955 at the Alvin Theatre. Produced by Maurice Evans in association with Emmett Rogers. Directed for the stage by Morton Da Costa. Written by Ira Levin. Adapted from the novel by Mac Hyman. With Andy Griffith as Will Stockdale, Roddy McDowall as Ben Whitledge, Myron McCormick as Sergeant King, Howard Freeman as General Bush, and Don Knotts as Manual Dexterity Corporal.

The story is almost legend now. Southern boy is drafted by the United States Air Force and doesn't mind—in fact, he thinks he's been honored, much to the horror and disbelief of his fellow officers. Mix in a best buddy, saluting toilets and a long suffering sergeant and the recipe for huge laughs is complete.

A smash hit, *Sergeants* was well received by public and critics alike. Brooks Atkinson, theatre critic for *The New York Times* had this to say of Andy's performance as Will Stockdale:
"Fortunately, the author and the producer have found the ideal man to play the part of Will Stockdale on stage. He is Andy Griffith, a tall, folksy Southerner with a shining face, a wide smile, curly hair, a sweet accent and a general glow of friendliness and native hospitality. Mr. Griffith does not have to condescend to Will Stockdale. All he has to do is walk on the stage and look the audience straight in the face. If the armed forces cannot cope with Will Stockdale, neither can the audience resist Andy Griffith."

A month later, Atkinson was still impressed enough to write a follow up article: "... *No Time For Sergeants* is the funniest comedy so far this season... (Mr. Griffith) is the ideal man to represent Will on a Broadway stage. Although his Southern accent is broad, he does not labor it. Everything about him rings true; nothing he does on the stage seems artificial or sentimental."

Critics questioned whether or not Andy would be able to go beyond Will Stockdale. Decades later, after a rich career playing a wide assortment of roles, Griffith commented on this apprehension:

".... that role seemed so specialized that it would be hard to tell whether the person who (played Will) and did it well would be able to do anything or be able to understand anything else—or whether that person was just that (character). I can understand that—and I'm glad it's not true. I've had a real good life. I'm grateful to Will Stockdale for it."

Destry Rides Again Opened April 23, 1959 at the Imperial Theatre. Produced by David Merrick in association with Max Brown. Production Directed and Choreographed by Michael Kidd. Music and Lyrics by Harold Rome. Book by Leonard Gershe. Based on the short story by Max Brand. Production designed by Oliver Smith. Musical Direction and Vocal Arrangements by Lehman Engel. Orchestrations by Philip J. Lang. Dance Music Arranged by Genevieve Pitot. With Andy Griffith as Destry, Dolores Gray as Frenchy, Scott Brady as Kent and Jack Prince as Wash.

The rough and tough western town of Bottleneck needs taming, and who better than famed gunfighter Thomas Jefferson Destry, Jr., son of the famous gunfighter and lawman. When Destry arrives, the town discovers him to be a peaceable fellow. He doesn't even wear a gun, until the end of the play where he must take up arms in a climactic gun battle. His life is saved by Frenchy, the top entertainer in the Last Chance Saloon, who has discovered she loves the new sheriff.

Robert Coleman of the *New York Mirror* noted: "*Destry Rides Again* is a rip-roaring rouser. It had the first-nighters cheering. Spontaneous outbursts of applause stopped the show on several occasions. The customers could hardly wait for the end of numbers to shout their approval. It was a triumphant preem for an exciting landmark in horse operas."

157

DISCOGRAPHY

A Face In The Crowd Capitol Records. April 1957. W872. "Main Title (A Face In The Crowd)," "Free Man In The Morning" (Budd Schulberg/Tom Glazer), "Fruit Salad Ferryboat" (Tom Glazer), "Old Fashioned Marriage," "Just Plain Folks," "Piano Melody: Free Man In The Morning-Just Plain Folks," "Mama Guitar" (Budd Schulberg/Tom Glazer), "Rock-A-Billy Rock" (Tom Glazer), "Just A Closer Walk With Thee," "March Montage" (Tom Glazer), "Vitajex Jingle" (Budd Schulberg/Tom Glazer), "Rain Fever and Elevator" (Tom Glazer), "A Face In The Crowd" (Budd Schulberg/Tom Glazer).

The soundtrack from the motion picture includes rockabilly tinged rousers performed by Andy, who is in character as Lonesome Rhodes. There are also instrumentals, advertising jingles, a calypso number and other tunes related to the film. Lyrics to the songs were composed by the writer of the screenplay, Budd Schulberg with musician Tom Glazer. Sheet music was available for "Mama Guitar," which was also released as a single.

Just For Laughs Capitol Records. March 1958. T962. "What It Was, Was Football" (Andy Griffith) "Silhouettes" (Frank C. Slay, Jr./ Bob Crewe. Special Material by Andy Griffith and Ainslie Pryor), "Opera Carmen" (Andy Griffith/ Dick Ryan), "There's No Time For Sergeants" (Marcille McRae/Cecil Rutherford), "Romeo And Juliet" (Andy Griffith), "Make Yourself Comfortable" (Bob Merrill. Special Material by Andy Griffith and Ainslie Pryor), "Swan Lake" (Andy Griffith), "Conversations With A Mule" (Bob Miller).

Andy's first comedy album collects his early material, including the legendary "What It Was, Was Football," "Opera Carmen," "Romeo And Juliet," and "Make Yourself Comfortable." Most of these routines had already been previously released by Capitol as either singles or extended players (EPs).

Andy Griffith Shouts The Blues And Old Timey Songs Capitol Records. January 1959. Produced by Tom Morgan. All Uncredited Songs Traditional/Adapted by Andy Griffith. "The Preacher And The Bear," "The House Of The Rising Sun" (Campbell), "How Long, How Long Blues" (Carr), "The Crawdad Song," "Good Morning Blues" (Rushing/Basie/Durham), "Pick A Bale Of Cotton," "Police Department Blues," "Little Maggie," "Careless Love," "Molly Darlin'," "I Want A Little Girl" (Mencher/Moll).

Andy sings a series of traditional blues songs, with only one comedy segment (the Griffith chestnut, "The Preacher And The Bear") instead of the mix featured on his earlier album for Capitol. In the liner notes, Andy credits his mother and other folks from the Mount Airy area for instilling his love of the form. He also notes that "... my friend Ainslie Pryor said that I was about the worst blues singer he ever heard. And I will admit that I'm not the best, but in all modesty I will have to say that I expect I'm the loudest."

In a 1994 interview, Andy remarked about his cover of "The House Of The Rising Sun" (as well as the entire album): "After I made that record, I thought, 'Lord God, what did I do!?' "

Destry Rides Again Decca Records. 1959. DL 9075. Original Broadway Recording. Music and Lyrics by Harold Rome. Musical Direction and Vocal Arrangements by Lehman Engel. Orchestrations by Philip J. Lang. Dance Music Arranged by Genevieve Pitot. "Overture" (Orchestra), "Bottleneck" (Chorus and Orchestra), "Ladies" (Dolores Gray and Girls), "Hoop-de-Dingle" (Jack Prince and Chorus), "Tomorrow Morning" (Andy Griffith), "Ballad of the Gun" (Andy Griffith and Jack Prince), "I Know Your Kind" (Dolores Gray), "I Hate Him" (Dolores Gray), "Rose Lovejoy Of Paradise Alley" (Male Ensemble).

"Anyone Would Love You" (Andy Griffith and Dolores Gray), "Once Knew A Fella" (Andy Griffith and Male Ensemble), "Every

Once In A While (Male Ensemble and Orchestra), "Fair Warning" (Dolores Gray), "Are You Ready Gyp Watson?" (Dolores Gray and Chorus), "Not Guilty" (Male Ensemble), "Only Time Will Tell" (Andy Griffith and Chorus), "Respectability" (Elizabeth Watts and Rose Lovejoy Girls), "That Ring On The Finger" (Dolores Gray, Rosetta LeNoire and Girls), "Once Knew A Fella" (Andy Griffith and Dolores Gray), "I Say Hello" (Dolores Gray), "Ballad Of The Gun Finale" (Chorus and Orchestra).

Andy's first album not on the Capitol label. Well recorded version of the Broadway musical.

This Here Andy Griffith Capitol Records. July 1959. T1215. Produced by Tom Morgan. "North Carolina, My Home State" (Andy Griffith), "Thank Heaven For Little Girls" (Alan Jay Lerner/ Fredrick Loewe), "Love Poems: To The Lovely Juanita Beasley" (Andy Griffith/Billy May), "Bad, Bad Business" (Joann Belvin), "Little Brown Church" (Larry Coleman), "Hamlet" (Andy Griffith), "Andy's Lament" (Hal Stanley/Kay Starr), "Love Poems: Togetherness" (Andy Griffith/Billy May), "St. James Infirmary" (Joe Primrose).

After the dearth of comedy on his last Capitol album, Andy returns to his usual mix of humorous monologues and music. The lead track, in which Andy speaks of his love of North Carolina (mentioning his father, Carl and going down to the Snappy Lunch for hot dogs) was recorded live at the annual banquet of the North Carolina Society in Washington, DC. On the vocal side, Andy's baritone is in fine form on a stirring rendition of "Little Brown Church," and he even manages to pull off a sincere version of "Thank Heaven For Little Girls."

The Andy Griffith Show Capitol Records. September, 1961. Produced by Tom Morgan. Orchestra Conducted by Earle Hagen. "The Andy Griffith Theme" (Earle Hagen/Herbert Spencer), "Jack, The Giant Killer" (Andy Griffith/Earle Hagen), "Flop Eared Mule"

(Traditional/Adapted by Andy Griffith), "Ellie's Theme" (Earle Hagen), "Sourwood Mountain" (Traditional/Adapted by Andy Griffith), "The Man Hunt" (Earle Hagen), "The Fishin' Hole" (Earle Hagen/Herbert Spencer/Everett Sloane), "Aunt Bee" (Earle Hagen), "The New River Train" (Traditional/Adapted by Andy Griffith), "Mayberry March" (Earle Hagen), "Cindy" (Traditional/Adapted by Andy Griffith), "Barney's Hoe Down" (Earle Hagen).

Soundtrack from the television series mixed with Andy singing some bluegrass and telling his monologue, "Jack, The Giant Killer." Hagen's music is a treat, allowing the listener to enjoy themes for Andy, Aunt Bee, and best of all, Barney Fife. The rarest of Griffith's Capitol albums.

Andy And Cleopatra Capitol Records. March 1964. T2066. Produced by Lee Gillette and Tom Morgan. "Andy and Cleopatra" (Aaron Ruben), "Let's Pull Together" (Bud Yorkin/Norman Lear), "A Good Man Is Hard To Find" (Edward Green), "The Discovery Of America" (Aaron Ruben), "Pool Table" (Charles R. Green), "Jack The Giant Killer" (Andy Griffith/Earle Hagen).

Six lengthy monologues (three per side) allow Griffith to get into telling a story, with "Andy and Cleopatra," "The Discovery of America" and "Jack The Giant Killer" (in case you missed it on the TV soundtrack) being the best tracks. The routines run the gamut, from live performances to in studio recordings backed by a lush symphony orchestra.

The Best Of Andy Griffith Capitol Records. T2707. "What It Was, Was Football Part I & II" (Andy Griffith), "The Discovery Of America" (Aaron Ruben),"The Preacher And The Bear" (Traditional Arrangement/Andy Griffith), "Romeo And Juliet" (Andy Griffith), "Pool Table" (Charles L. Green), "Andy And Cleopatra" (Aaron Ruben), "Love Poems: To The Lovely Juanita Beasley" (Andy Griffith/Billy May), "Opera Carmen" (Andy Griffith/Dick Ryan), "Don't Look Back" (Edward Dietrich/Michele Bertoia).

Somebody Bigger Than You And I Columbia Records, 1972. KC 31624. Produced by Billy Sherrill. Background Vocalists: The Jordanaires. Uncredited Songs Arranged by Billy Sherrill. "Somebody Bigger Than You And I" (J. Lange/H. Heath/S. Burke), "Take My Hand Precious Lord," "When They Ring The Golden Bells," "Just A Little Talk With Jesus," "Lead Me To That Rock," "Precious Memories," "Just A Closer Walk With Thee," "It Is No Secret" (S. Hamblen), "Turn Your Radio On" (A.E. Brumley), "I'll Fly Away" (A.E. Brumley), "I'm Gonna Write A Song" (G. Sutton).

Andy's personal favorite of his recordings. A beautiful album of straight gospel music, harkening back to Griffith's teenage years in Mount Airy and at Chapel Hill. Backed by longtime Elvis Presley vocalists the Jordanaires, Andy has never sounded better than when singing here in a rich bass voice with none of his southern twang.

Andy Griffith/American Originals Capitol Records. July 1992. CDP 0777 7 98476 2 4. Produced and Compiled by Jenny Bingaman. Digitally Remastered by Larry Walsh at Capitol Recording Studios, Hollywood. "The Fishin' Hole" (Hagen/ Spencer/Sloane), "What It Was, Was Football Part I & II" (Andy Griffith), "Cindy" (Traditional Arrangement/Andy Griffith), "Love Poems: To The Lovely Juanita Beasley" (Andy Griffith/Billy May), "Make Yourself Comfortable" (Bob Merrill/Special Material by Andy Griffith and Ainslie Pryor).

"North Carolina, My Home State" (Andy Griffith), "The Preacher And The Bear" (Traditional Arrangement/Andy Griffith), "Romeo And Juliet Part I & II" (Andy Griffith) "Love Poems: Togetherness" (Andy Griffith/Billy May), "Swan Lake" (Andy Griffith), "Flop Eared Mule" (Traditional Arrangement/Andy Griffith), "Hamlet" (Andy Griffith), "The Discovery Of America" (Aaron Ruben), "Don't Look Back" (Edward Dietrich/Michele Bertoia), "Opera Carmen" (Andy Griffith/Dick Ryan), "Andy And Cleopatra" (Aaron

Ruben), "The Midnight Special" (P. Campbell/J. Newman), "The Andy Griffith Theme" (Earle Hagen/H. Spencer).

A lovingly restored greatest hits album that collects most of the essential early Griffith comedy recordings.

SELECTED AWARDS & HONORS

1957   Key to the City, presented June 1 in Mount Airy on Andy's birthday by Mayor W. F. Carter. The city also celebrated the occasion as "Andy Griffith Day."

1961:   The Tarheel Award, presented in Washington, DC by then Secretary of Commerce and longtime Griffith friend, Luther Hodges.

1962:   The Distinguished Salesman's Award, given by a prominent group of civic leaders in Asheville, NC.

1968:   Outstanding Television Personality Of The Year, given by the Advertising Club of Baltimore.

1968:   National Brotherhood Award from the National Conference of Christians and Jews, given for "his concern for his fellowman and dedication for building a harmonious life for all people."

1969:   The Morrison Award for Excellence in the Performing Arts by a North Carolinian.

1969:   Doctor of Fine Arts title from Florida Southern College. When receiving the award, Andy joked, "This is pretty high on the hog for an old country boy who made mostly 'C's at the University of North Carolina."

1975:   Surry Arts Council names Andy Griffith Playhouse in Andy's honor.

1978:   Honorary Membership Chairman of the North Carolina Museum of History Associates—a group of volunteer and financial supporters for the North Carolina State Museum of History in Raleigh.

1978: Distinguished Alumnus Award from the University of North Carolina at Chapel Hill. "Andy Griffith may be the most widely known and recognized alumnus of this institution," said the presenter.

1983: The North Carolina Award For Fine Arts. Amusingly enough, it took Andy ten years until August of 1993 to finally accept the award formally in a ceremony held in Manteo where Governor Jim Hunt spoke of how Griffith's talent and generosity have enriched NC, and burnished its image.

1992: The Lifetime Achievement Award from the National Association of Television Programming Executives. The presentation was made by Ron Howard at the group's annual convention in New Orleans.

1992: Inducted into the Academy of Television Arts Hall of Fame at a ceremony held in Orlando, Florida. Don Knotts and George "Goober" Lindsay were presenters.

ENDORSEMENTS

Andy Griffith has never been reticent to lend his name and image to help promote a product. From shoes to soda pop to televisions and beyond, Andy's smiling face and warm demeanor has helped convince many a consumer to sample a company's wares. Since his career began with "What It Was, Was Football" the performer has been involved with a wide variety of goods and services, a selected group of which is listed below.

Andy Griffith Whole Hog Sausage, Andy Griffith Blackeyed Peas and Andy Griffith Navy Beans "G-o-o-o-o-d eatin' "

General Electric

Halo Shampoo "You Can Always Tell A Halo Girl"

Hess & Clark Products

AT&T "Relax."

Open Pit Barbecue Sauce

Post Toasties "Cracklin' fresh!"

Jomar Coffee

Suncrest Soda "Enter Andy's Big Orange Drink Contest"

Ritz Crackers "Mmmmmm—good cracker."

JELL-O Pudding

Kraft Cheese

167

BIBLIOGRAPHY

"After Setbacks, Griffith Finds Deep Happiness." *Winston-Salem Journal*, November 10, 1984.

"Alumni Profile: 'Preciating Andy Griffith, '49." *The University Of North Carolina At Chapel Hill Alumni Review*, November, 1978.

Amory, Cleveland. "Headliners." *This Week Magazine, 1967.*

Andrews, Jody. "The Secret Life Of A Married Man." *TV Radio Mirror*, September, 1963.

"Andy Griffith Likes Calling Manteo Home." *The Outer Banks Current*, October 25, 1989.

"Andy Griffith Looking Back." *Carolina View*, November/December 1985.

"Andy Griffith's Early Days." *The Mayberry Confidential*, September 27, 1991.

"Andy Is Mighty Proud To Return To Mayberry." *Winston-Salem Journal*, April 12, 1986.

Ardmore, Jane. "I Was A Born Loser." *Photoplay*, February, 1971.

Atkinson, Brooks. "Alvin Premiere For *No Time For Sergeants*." *The New York Times*, October 21, 1955.

Atkinson, Brooks. "Service Snafu." *The New York Times*, November 6, 1955.

Balling, Fredda. "Hillbilly Hero." *TV Radio Mirror*, October, 1957.

Beck, Ken. "Everyone's 'Nuts' About Don Knotts." *The Bullet*, August 27, 1983.

Beck, Marilyn. "Nothing Could Be Finer Than A Production In Carolina As Matlock Begins 8th Season." *The Star-Ledger*, August 1, 1993.

Beck, Marilyn. "Andy Griffith... Says He'll Never Say Never Again." *Entertainment Week*, July 24, 1993.

Berrier, R. J. "City Plans Huge Andy Day." *The Mount Airy Times*, May 31, 1957.

Bray, Jim. "The Bartered Bride." *The Mayberry Confidential*, September 27, 1991.

Brooks, Tim and Earle Marsh. *The Complete Directory To Prime Time*

Shows: Fifth Edition. New York: Ballantine Books, 1989.

Buck, Jerry. "I Was Paralyzed! What Was Wrong With Me?!" *Redbook*, May, 1989.

"Bumpkin To Big-Timer." *Newsweek*, January 18, 1954.

Castleman, Harry and Walter J. Podrazik. *Watching TV*. New York: McGraw-Hill Book Company, 1982.

Castleman, Harry and Walter J. Podrazik. *Harry And Wally's Favorite TV Shows*. New York: Pentrice Hall Press, 1989.

Chaffin, Tom. "It's A Mayberry State Of Mind." *The Detroit Free Press*, October, 1990.

Chiles, Kara. "Matlock In Camelot." *The Wilmington Star News*, August 29, 1993.

Clark, Jim. "News Of Cast And Crew." *The Bullet*, March 17, 1985.

Clark, Jim. "News Of Cast And Crew." *The Bullet*, February 15, 1992.

Clark, Jim. "Howard McNear—The Many Parts Of Floyd The Barber." *The Bullet*, June 1, 1992.

Clark, Jim. "News Of Cast And Crew." *The Bullet*, January 26, 1993.

Clark, Jim. "Jack Prince—Mayberry Star Still Shining." *The Bullet*, April 1993.

Clark, Jim. "Everett Greenbaum—A Man Whose Words Fly High In Mayberry." *The Bullet*, February 22, 1994.

Clarke, Jay. "Southern Roots Help Shape Careers." *Travel 50 And Beyond*, Spring, 1993.

Collins, Terry. "Music Was One Of Griffith's First Loves." *The Mount Airy News Progress Edition*, March 29, 1992.

Condon, Maurice. "He Never Left Home." *TV Guide*, June 4, 1966.

Cox, Tyler. "Andy Griffith Praised As Only Man To Ever Add Whole Town To NC—Mayberry." *The Mount Airy News*, October 13, 1978.

Crowther, Bosley. "Review: *No Time For Sergeants*." *The New York Times*, May 30, 1958.

Davidson, Bill. "Andy Griffith's $3,500,000 Misunderstanding." *TV Guide*, January 9, 1971.

Davis, Ivor. "Andy Griffith's Battle Back From Paralyzing Disease." *The Star*, September 30, 1986.

DeLaughter, Jerry. "Andy Griffith... Still At Home In Manteo." *The State*, November, 1987.

Demaret, Kent. "What It Is, Is The Tough Game Of TV Ratings That Veteran Andy Griffith Is Playing Again." *People Weekly*, 1979.

Denis, Paul. "Andy Griffith's Wife Talks About His Secret Vow! His Next Big Step! The Life They Share!" *TV Picture Life*, December, 1968.

Dern, Marian. "A Southern Sheriff Faces Some Problems." *TV Guide*, April 24, 1965.

"Doin' What Comes Natural." *TV Guide*, October 1, 1960.

"Eastward, Ever Eastward." *Newsweek*, October 23, 1961.

Edson, Lee. "Cornball With The Steel-Trap Mind" (Parts 1 & 2). *TV Guide*, February 3 & 10, 1961.

Elliott, Lawrence. "Andy Griffith: Yokel Boy Makes Good." *Coronet* October, 1957.

Esterly, Glenn. " 'Moving That Toe—It Beat Any Ovation I Ever Got.' " *TV Guide*, October 4, 1986.

Fishman, Charles. "A Few Moments With... Andy Griffith." *Florida Magazine*, January 10, 1993.

Freeman, Donald. "I Think I'm Gaining On Myself." *The Saturday Evening Post*, January, 1964.

Funk, Tim. "This Is Andy. Plain Spoken. Just Folks. Just Like You Expected." *The Charlotte Observer*, February 7, 1993.

Funk, Tim. "Not Much Changes In Town Of Mayberry." *The Greensboro News And Record*, September 27, 1994.

Gardella, Kay. "Homespun, But Not Like Old Times." *The New York Daily News*, April 11, 1986.

Goodman, Bob. "Andy Shooting For Another Series." *The Atlanta Journal*, April 13, 1974.

Griffith, Andy. Letter to Robert Smith, July 8, 1952. Mount Airy Visitor's Center Archives, Mount Airy, NC.

Griffith, Andy. Letter to Robert Smith, November 3, 1952. Mount Airy Visitor's Center Archives, Mount Airy, NC.

Griffith, Andy. Letter to Robert Smith, December 12, 1953. Mount Airy Visitor's Center Archives, Mount Airy, NC.

Griffith, Andy. Letter to Mayor W.F. Carter, Fall, 1957. Mount Airy Visitor's Center Archives, Mount Airy, NC.

Griffith, Andy. "We Got Lucky!" *Chicago Tribune TV Week*, September 23-29, 1961.

Griffith, Andy. Biographical essay for *The Player*. Reprinted in Discovering North Carolina: A Tar Heel Reader as "Andy Griffith Makes People Laugh." Ed. by Lillian and Helen Ross. 1960s.

Griffith, Andy. "Gentle Is The Word For North Carolina." *The Ford Times*, April, 1967.

Griffith, Andy. "Remembering Carolina." *The University Report*, September, 1983.

"Griffiths Say Good-Bye To Friendly City Today." *The Mount Airy News*, April 15, 1966.

Hall, Jane. "Going Home To Mayberry." *People Weekly*, April 14, 1986.

Hampton, Tim. "A Conversation With Andy Griffith." *The Greenville Independent*, May, 1993.

Harvey, Alec. "Andy's Career Beyond Mayberry." *The Birmingham News*, September 25, 1994.

Ed Hodges. "Andy Griffith: I Cannot Live Without Acting." *The Charlotte Observer*, November 26, 1992.

Hull, Bob. "Three Funny Men Reunited." *Los Angeles Herald-Examiner TV Weekly*, October 3-9, 1965.

" 'If It Becomes A Series, Can We Shoot At Malibu?' " *TV Guide*, April 20, 1974.

Inman, David. "What It Was Was *The Andy Griffith Show*." *VCR*, February, 1986.

Javna, John. *Cult TV*. New York: St. Martin's Press, 1985.

Jones, Tricia. "Everybody Was Laughing—But Me!" *TV Radio Mirror*, December, 1963.

Kelly, Richard. *The Andy Griffith Show*. Winston-Salem, NC: John F. Blair, 1981.

King, Bill. "Andy Griffith Changes His Image." *The Atlanta Constitution TV Week*, February 13, 1983.

King, Bill. "Memories Of Mayberry." *The Atlanta Constitution TV Week*, January 24, 1982.

King, Bill. "Twenty-Five Years Later, Mayberry's Never Looked So Good." *The Atlanta Constitution*, October 3, 1985.

King, Bill. "Andy Griffith Can't Be Beaten By Pain." *The Atlanta Constitution*, March 3, 1986.

King, Susan. "Mayberry On Their Minds." *The Los Angeles Times*, February 6, 1993.

Klein, Andy. "*Hearts Of The West*" (Video Review). *American Film*, February, 1991.

Krupnick, Jerry. "Star Andy Griffith Taking *Matlock* One Hour At A Time." *The Star Ledger*, January 12, 1993.

Lawrence, Keith. "Well, Golly! A Real-Life 'Mayberry?' " *Winston-Salem Journal*, December 27, 1984.

Leahy, Jack. "Doin' What Comes Natcherly." *The New York Sunday Times*, January 21, 1962.

Leahy, Michael. "Case Closed." *TV Guide*, November 17, 1990.

Leonard, John. "Blurred Vision." *New York*, November 26, 1984.

Levin, Steve. "Andy Of Manteo." *Carolina Lifestyle*, June, 1983.

Lewis, Richard Warren. "The Wondrous Andy Griffith TV Machine" (Parts 1 & 2) *TV Guide*, July 13 & 20, 1968.

Linke, Richard O. "Biography: Andy Griffith." Unpublished Client Biography. July 21, 1984.

Long, Margaret. "Socials And Personals" (Society Column). *The Goldsboro News Argus*, September 12, 1949.

Lowry, Cynthia. "Berry Is Replacing Griffith." *Winston-Salem Journal*, Fall, 1969.

Lucas, Bob. "Loner, Worrier And Door-Puncher." *TV Radio Mirror*, August, 1967.

"Man With A Dream." *The Whittier California Daily News TV Week*, June 3, 1979.

Marill, Alvin H. *Movies Made For Television: The Telefeature And The Mini-Series 1964-1986*. New York: A Baseline Book, 1987.

"*Matlock* Gets Some Help This Fall." *The Mount Airy News TV Week*, July 11 to July 17, 1987.

Mayfield, Mark. "*Matlock* Jury Stacked With Fans." *USA Today*, January 13, 1993.

McAllister, Jim. "Running Scared." *TV Guide*, October 16, 1971.

McManus, Margaret. "Griffith Relieved By Switch From Headmaster To Mayor." *Winston-Salem Journal*, January 24, 1971.

McNeil, Alex. *Total Television*. New York: Penguin Books USA, 1980.

Mickey, Edward T. "The Andy Griffith I Know." *The Wachovia Moravian*, February 1968.

Milne, Tom, Ed. *The Time Out Film Guide*. New York: Penguin Books USA, 1991.

Merrill, Don. "*Matlock*" (Review). *TV Guide*, December 20, 1986.

Millstein, Gilbert. "Strange Chronicle Of Andy Griffith." *The New York Times Magazine*, June 2, 1957.

Mitz, Rick. *The Great TV Sitcom Book*. New York: Perigee Books, 1988.

Neal, Patricia. *As I Am*. New York: Simon and Schuster, 1988.

North Carolina People with William Friday. The University of North Carolina for Public Broadcasting. Interview with Griffith. December, 1993.

No Time For Sergeants. Rhino Home Video/The Golden Age Of Television. Interview with Griffith and Ira Levin. 1955/1993.

Peary, Danny. *Alternate Oscars*. New York: Delta Books, 1993.

Peary, Danny. *Guide For The Film Fanatic*. New York: Fireside Books/Simon and Schuster, 1986.

"People Picks And Pans: *Murder In Texas*" (Review). *People Weekly*, May 4, 1981.

Pfeiffer, Lee. *The Official Andy Griffith Show Scrapbook*. New York: Citadel Press, 1994.

Purcelli, Marion. "Corn Pone Comedian." *Chicago Tribune TV Week*, October 17-23, 1964.

Purcelli, Marion. "All About Mayberry." *Chicago Tribune TV Week*, October 28-November 3, 1967.

Quinn, Christopher. "Memory: Cousin Recalls Andy Griffith's Boyhood." *Winston-Salem Journal*, September 30, 1990.

Raddatz, Leslie. "Aneta Corsaut." *TV Guide*, May 20, 1967.

Rader, Dotson. "Why I Listened To My Father." *Parade*, February 4, 1990.

Reynolds, Debbie and David Patrick Columbia. *Debbie*. New York: William Morrow and Company, 1988.

Robertson, Mildred. "Rememberin' Andy." *The Mayberry Confidential*, September 27, 1991.

Rubin, Sam. "Andy Griffith: My Nightmare Battle With Mystery Illness." *The National Enquirer*, June 7, 1983.

Sackett, Susan. *The Hollywood Reporter Book Of Box Office Hits*. New York: Billboard Publications, 1990.

Schenck, Anne. "What It Was, Was Andy." *Tarheel*, December, 1977.

Sherill, Martha. "Mount Airy, Adoring Andy." *The Washington Post*, October 1, 1990.

Spignesi, Stephen J. *Mayberry My Hometown*. Ann Arbor, Michigan: Popular Culture, Ink., 1987.

Story, David. *America On The Rerun*. New York: Citadel Press, 1993.

Teater, Robin P. "Taking *Matlock* To Mayberry." *The Daily News*, August 28, 1989.

Terrace, Vincent. *Television 1970-1980*. California: A.S. Barnes and Company, 1981.

"The Hillbilly's A Hit." *Newsweek*, October 31, 1955.

"The Show That Has H.A.Q." *TV Guide*, May 11, 1963.

Thompson, Estes. "Andy Griffith Says Acting All He Can Do." *The Mount Airy News*, October 13, 1994.

Weiler, A.H. "*Onionhead*" (Review). *The New York Times*, October 2, 1958.

"What It Is, Is Talk." *Time*, January 18, 1954.

"Who It Was, Was A Man They Call Andy Griffith." *Downbeat*, February 24, 1954.

Zuanich, Barbara. "Andy's New Wife." *Los Angeles Herald-Examiner TV Weekly*, January 17, 1971.

We hope you enjoyed reading *The Andy Griffith Story.*

If you know of others who are also fans of Mr. Griffith, additional copies are available from the publisher.

P.O. Box 1907   Mount Airy, NC 27030

Yes! I would like to order *The Andy Griffith Story*

Please send me _____ copies of the hardcover edition @ $23.95

Please send me _____ copies of the softcover edition @ $12.95

For postage and handling add $3.00 for the first book, plus $1.00 for each additional book. Allow four to six weeks for delivery.

I enclose a check or money order payable to Explorer Press in the amount of $ _____ (NC residents add 6% sales tax)

Name _____

Street Address _____

City _____

State _____ Zip _____

Phone _(_____)_____

For quotes on quantity purchases, please write Explorer Press, P.O. Box 1907, Mount Airy, NC 27030 (910) 789-3099.